D1075704
emon
Next Door
04
ory & art by Izumo Ito

SHAMIKO
SHAMIKO (YOSHIDA YUKO)
A demon who's gotten just a little bit stronger.
CHIYODA MOMO
CHIYODA MOMO
Shamiko's vassal (temporary).
FAVORITE FOOD
I don't really have one. Most foods are delicious!
FAVORITE QUOTE
None, really. If I had to pick one, maybe, "You win some; you lose some!"
FAVORITE FOOD
Lately it's been udon.
FAVORITE QUOTE
"Speak softly and carry a big stick."

I NEED A SPECIAL "QUEEN OF DARKNESS" MOVE!
I'VE BEEN GETTING CHASED A LOT ...
SO IT WOULD BE NICE TO HAVE A SPECIAL ATTACK WHEN I GET CORNERED.

YOU KNOW, LIKE "SHADOW SOMETHING-OR-OTHER"!
SHAMIKO'S ROUTINE: MAKE A WRONG MOVE, GET CHASED AROUND.
BEFORE WE PICK A NAME ...
WE SHOULD FIND A MOVE YOU CAN PULL OFF RELIABLY.

LIKE A BEAM, OR A PUNCH, OR A LEG-LOCK.
UM... DOES DOING IT IN DREAMS COUNT?
LET'S STICK TO REALITY.

......
......
THE ONLY MOVE I CAN PULL OFF RELIABLY IS CRYING.
"SHADOW SOB FEST" IT IS, THEN!

THE PROBLEM IS YOU PANIC WHEN YOU'RE IN TROUBLE.
YOU HAVE TO BE MORE RESPONSIVE.
GRAB
LET'S PRACTICE.
AAH, I DON'T LIKE WHERE THIS IS GOING!

FIRST, IF SOMEONE GRABS YOUR COLLAR, DO THIS!!
MEEP!
IF THEY FLY INTO A RAGE, KNOCK THEM OUT LIKE THIS!!
NU-WA-AH!

I CAN'T STOP MY SHADOW SOB FEST.
SNAP
NOW, WHAT DID WE LEARN TODAY?

OF COURSE, OPPONENTS WON'T USE MARTIAL ARTS MOVES, SO NONE OF THAT IS USEFUL.
FORGET IT ALL FOR NOW.
CURSE YOU!

LICO
LICO-KUN
A Chinese fox spirit. Can't take a hint.
SHIROSAWA
SHIROSAWA
Clearly a baku (or tapir), but also a gentleman.
BIRTHDAY/BLOOD TYPE
Mmm...no idea.
ROMANTIC PREFERENCE
Someone useful.
FAVORITE QUOTE
"The way to someone's heart is through their stomach," y'know!
BIRTHDAY/BLOOD TYPE
I'm sorry, I don't know.
ROMANTIC PREFERENCE
Female baku, I suppose.
FAVORITE QUOTE
"Hardship makes the man."

A SPECIAL ATTACK? MY COMBAT ABILITIES AREN'T VERY STRONG.
I *DO* HAVE ONE SPECIAL TALENT, THOUGH.

WE BAKU EXCEL AT PREDICTIONS AND FORTUNE-TELLING.*
THERE MAY BE GOLD THERE.
OOOH!
BACK WHERE I CAME FROM...
I MADE A LIVING TELLING FORTUNES FOR IMPORTANT FOLK.

IF YOU WANT TO KNOW MORE, PLEASE GOOGLE "BAI-ZE."
FORTUNE-TELLING?! I'D LOVE TO SEE THAT!!
I'M PAST MY PRIME, BUT... VERY WELL.

YOU WILL LOSE CONFIDENCE.
AMAZING! IT'S TRUE!!
PEOPLE SAY YOU DON'T KNOW HOW TO SAY NO.
WOWZERS!! IT'S *ALL* TRUE!!
SHAMIKO-HAN'S A SIMPLE GAL.

I DON'T HAVE A "SPECIAL MOVE" OR NOTHING...
BUT I DID HAVE AN ACE UP MY SLEEVE WHEN I FOUGHT THOSE MIKO-HAN.
W-WOULD YOU MIND SHOWING ME?

MMM... MAYBE NOT WITH MOMO-HAN HERE.
Y'KNOW... JUST IN CASE THE TIME EVER COMES...
ARE YOU *EXPECTING* THAT TIME TO COME?

OH, HEY! I GOT A SIMPLE ONE I CAN SHOW YA.
HERE, MOMO-HAN, DRINK *THIIIS!* ♪
I'M NOT DRINKING ANYTHING IN THOSE COLORS.

CAN'T BLAME YA~!
SAY, MOMO-HAN... COULD YOU BRING ME THAT CUP RIGHT OVER THERE?
CARE TO EXPLAIN THE OBVIOUS PITFALL TRAP FIRST?

**Shirosawa is using a traditional form of fortunetelling involving an ancient Chinese book called the* I Ching.

OGURA SION
OGURA SION
A mad scientist who appears when you least expect her.
SATA ANRI
SATA ANRI
She does her own thing but takes good care of her friends.

BIRTHDAY/BLOOD TYPE

December 14, type A.
People always assume I'm type B, though.
I wonder why?

HOBBIES

Reading, watching movies, observing people.

FAVORITE QUOTE

"Fortune favors the prepared mind."

BIRTHDAY/BLOOD TYPE

May 1, type O!

HOBBIES

Soft tennis* and BBQ.
Let's fire up the grill!

FAVORITE QUOTE

"Tomorrow is another day."
I just came up with that!

**Soft tennis is a Japanese variant on tennis played with soft rubber balls.*

A SPECIAL MOVE? SHOULDN'T YOU BUILD UP YOUR STAMINA FIRST, SHAMIKO?
WAIT... DID YOU COME JUST TO ASK ME THAT?
I'M HELPING OUT WITH THE FAMILY BIZ RIGHT NOW.

TO BUILD STAMINA, YA GOTTA EAT MEAT!!
FOR RUNNING, MEAT! FOR PUNCHING, MEAT!!
MEAT
WE'VE GOT SOME GREAT POULTRY IN TODAY!
IT'S SUPER FRESH!! THIS IS A ONCE-IN-A-LIFETIME CHANCE!!

UM... OKAY. TWO HUNDRED GRAMS, PLEASE.
TWOOO HUNDRED? OR THREEE HUNDRED??
UMM... THREE HUNDRED.

YOU WANT POWER, DON'T-CHA?
'CAUSE IF YOU DOOO...
HEH HEH HEH HEH HEH...
I, UM... FOUR HUNDRED GRAMS, PLEASE.
HEH HEH HEH HEH...
THIS IS ANRI-CHAN'S SPECIAL MOVE: THE MEAT-'EM-UP SPECIAL.

HOW'S IT GOING?
A SPECIAL MOVE... LIKE A KILLER ATTACK?
I'M SO THRILLED YOU CAME TO ME ABOUT THAT, SHAMIKO-CHAN.

I'LL TEACH YOU MY SPECIAL MOVE: ORGANIC SYNTHESIS!!
WOW, WHAT A GREAT ATTACK NAME!!

FIRST, YOU IMPORT SOME ■■■ FROM ■■■
THEN YOU SLOOOWLY MIX IT WITH HIGH-PURITY ■■■
BORROW SOME ■■■ AND ■■■ FROM THE SCIENCE LAB, THEN ■■■ THE VAPOR.
NEXT, YOU EVAPORATE THE ■■■...

AND VOILÀ! YOU'VE GOT SPECIAL-ATTACK POWDER AND THE LAW CAN'T TOUCH YOU!
LET'S GO HOME.
GOOD IDEA!! DINNER IS CHICKEN-FRIED STEAK TONIGHT!!

THE DEMON GIRL NEXT DOOR

CHARACTER RELATIONSHIP DIAGRAM

MAGICAL GIRLS
"SHE NEEDS MORE VITAMIN C."
TRUSTS
CHIYODA MOMO
WANTS TO DEFEAT
"WHAT'S FOR DINNER TODAY?"
YOSHIDA FAMILY
DREAM WORLD
BELOVED DESCENDANT
ADMIRATION
LILITH
HINATSUKI MIKAN
"SHE'S SO GIRLY AND NICE!"
"SHE NEEDS MORE CITRUS."
SHAMIKO
DRINKING BUDDY
SACRED OBJECT
COMMANDER-IN-CHIEF
SMART LITTLE SISTER
GOOD IN A PINCH
A GOOD RESEARCH SUBJECT FRIEND
RYOKO & SEIKO
"HOW'S IT GOIN'?"
SLOW AND STEADY
"ANY GAL WITH A TAIL IS A FRIEND OF MINE."
"I WANT TO FLUFF HER TAIL."
"CAN YOU WORK SATURDAY?"
A KINDLY BOSS
OGURA SION
SHIROSAWA
SATA ANRI
"HE'S AWFUL HANDY!"
EMPLOYEE
"CONTROL YOURSELF, GIRL!"
A FRIEND
LICO
CLASSMATES
CAFÉ ASURA

ESTIVAL
ESTIVAL
FESTIVAL
The Demon Girl Next Door 04
story & art by Izumo Ito
BENTO BOX 350 YEN
BENTO BOX 350 YEN
BENTO BOX 350 YEN

JULY X, SUNNY.
WE SEARCHED THE OLD FACTORY AND FOUND MY SEALED FATHER'S LOST WEAPON!

AUGUST X, DARK.
I GOT LOST IN MY OWN MEMORIES, AND MY MORTAL ENEMY FELL INTO DARKNESS TO SAVE ME.

AUGUST X-X, WEATHER UNKNOWN.
I ATE SOME MIND-ERASING FOOD AT WORK, SO I'M DRAWING A BLANK.

WHOA, SHAMIKO, YOUR SUMMER DIARY'S HOT STUFF!!
NICE CHIYO-MOMO DRAWING, TOO.
This isn't what I intended...
OUR MID-SUMMER SCHOOL CHECK-IN STARTS TODAY!

HOT LIKE RAMEN

IT'S BEEN TOUGH...
BUT I WANT TO TRY GATHER-ING MORE DARK VASSALS.
ANRI-CHAN, WOULD YOU MIND HELPING ME, PLEASE?

I'M HAPPY TO HELP...
BUT LISTEN, SHA-MIKO.
ARE YOU GETTING ENOUGH REST?
HUH?

UM, WELL... I'VE HAD A VERY INTENSE SUMMER BREAK.
THAT DOESN'T MEAN IT WAS REST-FUL!
YOUR DIARY IS FULL OF DISAS-TERS!

MOST HIGH-SCHOOL GIRLS DON'T INHERIT WEAPONS OVER SUMMER BREAK!
I...!! I GUESS YOU'RE RIGHT!
YOU SHOULD TRY TO TAKE THINGS DOWN A NOTCH!!

SHAMIKO'S SUMMER ASSESSMENT

IT ALSO SAYS YOU WOUND UP BEDRIDDEN TWICE, AND YOU LOST YOUR MEMORIES AT THE CAFÉ I RECOMMENDED! I FEEL RE-SPONSIBLE!
WHY DON'T YOU AT LEAST TAKE A DAY OFF?
ALSO, WHO KEEPS A DIARY LIKE THIS ANYMORE?
Japonica Workbook

WHERE'S CHIYO-MOMO?
SHE'S MEETING WITH MIKAN-SAN... THE BACKUP MAGICAL GIRL.
OKAY, I'LL GET IN TOUCH WITH HER.

SO, YOU JUST TAKE THE REST OF THE DAY OFF!
ENJOY A NICE, PROPER SUMMER BREAK!
A "PROPER SUMMER BREAK"?!

BUT... I'M A DEMON, SO--
LOOK, YOU ONLY GET ONE SUMMER TO BE FIFTEEN!
VIVA LA SUMMER VACATION!

STRATEGY GAME MISFIRE

GAME-OFF
TAMA STORE
Unplanned days off are the best way to recharge your batteries!
I ENDED UP TAKING A SURPRISE DAY OFF.
THIS TABLE 100 YEN

MOMOOOO!
HUH?
ガラ CLATTER リ
MOMO AND MIKAN LEFT AFTER THEIR MEETING.

THEY BORE ENORMOUS DUMBBELLS AND RUBBER TIRES--IN THIS HEAT!
TRYING TO GET MOMO'S MAGIC BACK, I BELIEVE.
OH... I SEE.
WHAT A PAIR OF FREAKS.

WAIT... DIDST THOU WISH TO JOIN THEM?
HUH?! N-NO!!
I'M... I'M JUST GLAD THEY DIDN'T DRAG ME ALONG!
はっ!!
ACK!!

ANCESTOR'S STARK SUGGESTION

THIS DOESN'T FEEL QUITE RIGHT.
ANCESTOR...WHAT WOULD YOU CALL A "PROPER SUMMER BREAK"?
HMM.

ALLOW ME TO THINK.
WE DID NOT HAVE "SUMMER BREAK" IN MESOPOTAMIA...
JUST THE DRY SEASON AND THE RAINY SEASON.

THE DRY SEASON WAS HOT ENOUGH TO SLAY ONE...
SO IT FELTETH GREAT TO NAP IN THE SHADE--STARK NAKED!
TRY AGAIN, PLEASE!
MESOPOTAMIA:
A LAWLESS LAND

DRINKING WINE... IN THE SHADE... STARK NAKED.
THAT'S EVEN WORSE!
I'LL JUST GO FOR A WALK!

YA GOTTA WORK HARDEST IN THE OFF-SEASON

HANG ON, I DON'T THINK THIS IS RIGHT!
YUKO-HAN, YOU'RE A GOOD SPORT.
YES, YOU WENT ALONG WITH THAT FOR QUITE A WHILE.
GRR!!

BUT YOU REALLY WERE A BIG HELP. HERE'S YOUR PAY FOR TODAY'S WORK.
OH... THANK YOU VERY MUCH!

WE'RE HAVING A "COOL-OFF FESTIVAL" IN THE SHOPPING CENTER.
THAT'S WHAT WE WERE SELLING THOSE BENTO BOXES FOR.
A FESTIVAL ?!
FESTIVAL
COOL
TAMA SAKURA SHOPPING DISTRI

FESTIVALS ARE A BATTLEGROUND FOR FOOD SERVICE!
THEY MOCK THE VERY CONCEPT OF VACATION!
SORRY I COULDN'T BE OF MORE HELP.
IT'S OKAY. UM, I'M SORRY, TOO.
GLINT...

A BREAK (OR NOT)

CAFE ASURA
'SCUSE ME~!
O-HO?
CAME FOR A VISIT, HUN? HOW NIIICE!

I HEARD ABOUT SAKURA-HAN. DON'T GIVE UP NOW, Y'HEAR?
HERE, THIS ONE'S ON THE BOSS.
LICO-KUN, DON'T GIVE OUT FREE FOOD IN MY NAME!
THIS TIME'S FINE, THOUGH !!

BOSS, LICO-SAN... WHAT'S A "PROPER SUMMER BREAK" LIKE?
A STUDENT'S SUMMER BREAK IS ALL ABOUT ...
THE GLORIOUS SWEAT OF GOOD, HONEST WORK!

NOW, THIS IS A REAL SUMMER BREAK!!
BENTO BOX LUNCHES FOR SALE!
GET YOUR BENTO BOX LUNCHES HEEERE !!
WAIT, NO IT'S NOT.
BENTO BOX 350 YEN
BENTO BOX 350 YEN

NO LOSING TICKETS

SAY, A FESTIVAL'S QUITE THE SUMMER BREAK STAPLE! WHY DON'TCHA COME?
I'LL GETCHA INTO A YUKATA,* EVEN!
OH GOSH, ARE YOU SURE?!

LOOKIN' GOOOOD!
THANK YOU SO MUCH!

I FEEL LIKE A RICH OIL TYCOON!
I'M GONNA LIVE IT UP!
NOW, THAT'S THE SPIRIT!

THERE'LL BE A TOY RAFFLE TOO, SO YOU SHOULD GO FOR BROKE ON THAAAT!
LICO-KUN, STOP THAT!
SHAMIKO-KUN, STAY AWAY FROM THAT RAFFLE!

A PROPER SUMMER BREAK

CLENCH
FRANKFURTERS
TAMA SAKURA
COOL
OKAY, LET'S HAVE SOME FUUUN!
ICE

COTTON CANDY 500 YEN EACH
WHEEEE!
AH HA HA HA... HA...

GRILLED CHICKE
HRRRM...
?
HUNH... THIS STILL DOESN'T FEEL RIGHT.
MY TAIL'S ALL DROOPY... BUT WHY?
ICE ICE ICE ICE

I'VE GOT ALL THESE SUPER-SUMMERY ITEMS, AND YET...
IT ALL FEELS SO EMPTY. WHY?!
ARE DEMONS JUST NOT MEANT TO ENJOY SUMMER?!

* A yukata is a casual, unlined summer kimono worn by men and women. It is usually made of light material such as cotton.

ARE ANY TRAITS BESIDES "HORNS" NECESSARY?

IT JUST... DOESN'T FEEL FUN, ALL BY MYSELF.
I WONDER WHY?
I NEVER MINDED BEING ALONE BEFORE.
RAFFLE
RAFFLE
RAFFLE

MAYBE I'LL JUST GO HOME.
BANANA
TAIYAKI
Next, we have a lost child report.

From Tama City ...
fifteen-year-old Shadow Mistress Yuko-chan.
?!
She's small, with wavy hair and curved horns.

WHAT THE HECK WAS THAT?!
Her subordinates are looking for her.
Please report any sightings to the info desk.
BOW WOW!! !

DRESS CODE JUTSU

WHO'S MAKING RUDE ANNOUNCEMENTS ABOUT ME?!
SHAMIKO! WE'VE BEEN LOOKING FOR YOU!
INFO
I KNEW IT, MAGICAL GIRL!

I'M NOT A LOST LITTLE KID, YOU KNOW!
AND DON'T CALL ME "SMALL" EVER AGAIN!
THE "SUBORDINATES" PART FELT NICE, THOUGH!

WAIT, WHA--?
YUKATA?
OH, RIGHT.

WE LOOKED FOR YOU AT THE CAFÉ AND THIS HAPPENED.
SHE'S SOMEHOW MADE IT SO WE CAN'T TAKE THEM OFF.
They'll come off at midnight~!
O-OH, I SEE!

YOU'RE GOING HOME?

WE HEARD YOU WANTED TO TAKE A BREAK ...
BUT IT'S SO HOT OUT, WE GOT A BIT WORRIED.
EHEH!
O-OH, IS THAT RIGHT?
EHEH!
THEN, I GUESS--

SO SORRY FOR DISRUPTING YOUR DAY OFF.
LET'S GO HOME, MIKAN. THIS OUTFIT IS EMBARRASSING.
WHA ...!
WAIT!
GRAB

?
YOU'RE GONNA RUN AWAY FROM SUMMER, HUH?
SO MUCH FOR THE LIGHT CLAN!
GRRR!

WHAT DO YOU MEAN, "RUN AWAY FROM SUMMER"?
FORGET THAT!
LET'S JUST USE UP SOME SUMMER BEFORE YOU GO HOME!

A DEMON WHO CAN ENJOY SUMMER?

APRICOT CANDY
LET'S GO! HURRY IT UP!

HUNH! NOW THIS FEELS RIGHT.
WHAT DO YOU MEAN?

I GUESS DEVOURING SUMMER ALONE ...
WAS IMPOSSIBLE FOR A SMALL-SCALE DEMON LIKE ME.
SUMMER IS ABOUT SHARING ENERGY...

SO A DEMON SHOULD SHARE SUMMER WITH HER SUBORDINATES!
EAT THIS! DEMON TAKOYAKI!
WHY IS SHE SO HUNG UP ON THIS SUMMER THING?

STAY AWAY FROM THAT RAFFLE

LET'S DO THIS AGAIN SOMETIME!
YES, LET'S!
We have another call for a guest:

Black-hearted Magical Girl Fresh Peach.
The singing, dancing, adorable, haunted doll Lilith-chan...
about five thousand years old, is looking for you.

THAT BLASTED RAFFLE!! I DIDN'T WIN ONCE!!
MOMO, HURRY HITHER!
INFO
PLEASE BRING FRESH FUNDS TO THE INFORMATION DESK AT ONCE!

WHAT THE HECK WAS THAT?
……
?

I DON'T KNOW HER

IS MY ANCESTOR HERE, TOO?
……
SHE WANTED A PRIZE, SO I GAVE HER SOME POCKET MONEY AND LEFT HER THERE.
RAFFLE 300 YEN
CUP CAKES

Fresh Peach from Tama City, please bring fresh funds.
HUNH, I WONDER WHO THEY'RE LOOKING FOR.
BUT "FRESH PEACH" IS *YOUR* TITLE, ISN'T IT, MOMO?

NO? I DON'T KNOW HER.
SMILE...
A CUTE SMILE WON'T GET YOU OUT OF THIS!!

ONCE THE ENERGY IN HER HOST BODY RUNS OUT...
HER SOUL WILL RETURN TO THE STATUE.
WE SHOULD GO GET HER ANYWAY!
DON'T GIVE UP, SHAMIKO! HAVE LOTS OF FUN AND LIVE A LIFE FULL OF WORK AND PLAY!

NNGH... AAGH... UUGH...
WHAT, ARE YOU HUNGRY?
MATH I-A
THAT'S NOT IT!

I'M TRYING TO DO MY SUMMER HOMEWORK.
I'VE BEEN SO BUSY I HAVEN'T GOTTEN FAR.
MATH I-A
100 Basic Problems

SO, YOU'RE A DEMON WHO DOES HER HOMEWORK. GOOD FOR YOU!
I HAVEN'T EVEN STARTED MINE.
OF COURSE! I AM A FINE YOUNG DEMON!

......
WAIT, WHAT ?!
THAT'S AWFUL!! YOU'RE SUPPOSED TO BE THE GOOD ONE!!
ぱっ!!
JOLT

OVERQUALIFIED FOR FALLING INTO DARKNESS

YOU HAVEN'T STARTED YOUR HOMEWORK?!
BUT YOU'RE SO SMART!
I MEAN, THAT'S NOT THE REASON, EXACTLY...

I JUST LEFT ALL THE WORKSHEETS SHOVED INTO MY DESK, YOU FEEL ME?
NO, I DON'T "FEEL YOU"!
THIS MAKES NO SENSE!

SO, I GUESS I KINDA FIGURED, "OH WELL... NO BIGGIE."
IT'S A SUPER-BIG BIGGIE!!
WHAT KIND OF MAGICAL GIRL DOESN'T DO HER HOMEWORK?!

THE KIND WHO TEMPORARILY FELL INTO DARKNESS, MAYBE?
THAT'S NO EXCUSE AND YOU KNOW IT!!

PEACH BUTTON-PUSHER

IT'S FINE. I'LL JUST TAKE A STEP-BY-STEP APPROACH.
AND WHAT'S THE FIRST STEP?!
YOU KNOW, LIKE... STEPS.
LOOK ME IN THE EYE AND TELL ME!
SHAKE SHAKE
SHAKE SHA

COME TO THINK OF IT, MOMO ALWAYS LEAVES HER TESTS SHOVED IN HER DESK, TOO.
IF MY (TEMP) VASSAL IS IN TROUBLE...
THEN I'VE GOT TO HELP HER OUT!
SHE CAN BE SLOPPY SOMETIMES.

MOMO! LET'S DO OUR HOMEWORK TOGETHER!
IF WE FINISH THE PROBLEMS AND REVIEW OUR NOTES...
WE SHOULDN'T HAVE ANY TROUBLE WITH THE BACK-TO-SCHOOL EXAMS.

BUT YOU'LL HAVE TROUBLE NO MATTER WHAT, WON'T YOU?
GRRRAAAAHH!!
YOU REALLY ARE MY ARCHENEMY!!

LOGICAL MAGICAL GIRL

BESIDES, WHY DO WE GET HOMEWORK FOR SUMMER "BREAK"?
HUH? 'CAUSE SCHOOL IS SUPPOSED TO TEACH US STUFF.
BUT I PAY ATTENTION IN CLASS AND LEARN EVERYTHING THERE.

CALLING IT A "BREAK," YET GIVING US WORK...
ISN'T THAT BASICALLY ILLEGAL STUDY LABOR?
WHAT'S "STUDY LABOR"?

SHAMIKO, TO ELIMINATE ILLEGAL "S. L." FROM THIS TOWN...
SHOULDN'T YOU FIGHT IT WITH PHYSICAL TRAINING?
I... UM... MAYBE? IS THAT RIGHT?
CLASP

I'LL USE MY MUSCLES TO PROTECT YOU THIS SUMMER BREAK.
NOW, CAST ASIDE YOUR BOOKS AND LET'S GO!
O...OKAY!!
SHAMIKO, COLLECT THYSELF!! FALL NOT FOR HER FAULTY LOGIC!

I TOLD YOU NOT TO CALL ME SMALL

WHY ARE YOU SO FIXATED ON MY HOMEWORK?

S-SAKURA-SAN ASKED ME TO LOOK AFTER YOU!

SINCE I'VE GOT HER CORE ON LOAN RIGHT NOW.

IN FACT...THINK OF ME AS A SUBSTITUTE BIG SISTER!
I HATH BEEN BRIBED!
YOU ARE MY (TEMP) VASSAL, AFTER ALL!

BIG SISTER?
BWA-HAAA!
HRMM...

NOPE, DON'T SEE IT.
HEY! LET'S TAKE THIS TO THE RIVERBANK!
I'LL MAKE YOU TREAT ME AS A REAL ARCH-ENEMY!

MOMO'S ORIGIN, REVEALED!

BESIDES... MY SISTER ALWAYS DID HER HOMEWORK AT THE LAST MINUTE, TOO.
WHAAAAT?!
OH... THAT ACTUALLY DOES KINDA MAKE SENSE.

APPARENTLY, I WAS AN ORPHAN.
WHA--?
I DON'T REMEMBER MUCH...
BUT MY SISTER SAID I HAD POTENTIAL AS A MAGICAL GIRL AND TOOK ME IN.

I WAS PRETTY SHY AT FIRST...
SO SHE TOOK ME ALONG WITH HER A LOT. AND I REMEMBER...

SHE WOULD FREAK OUT LAST-MINUTE OVER A MOUNTAIN OF HOMEWORK.
AAAAAH!!
THE TIME... TIME... TIME...
A
A
A
SHE'S THE TYPE WHO FLIES BY THE SEAT OF HER PANTS.

ONIGIRI ARE YUMMY

Momo-chan, deadlines can stretch like a rubber band.
I'll go apologize to the teacher.
Got it.
SEE?
THAT'S THE WRONG LESSON!

HOMEWORK IS A PROMISE TO YOUR TEACHERS!
AND IT'S IMPORTANT TO KEEP YOUR PROMISES!
SIT! SIT, I SAY!
I'LL WATCH YOU WHILE YOU DO YOUR HOMEWORK TODAY.

AW, WHAT...?
YOU WON'T BE SLEEPING TONIGHT!!
THIS IS PAYBACK FOR THAT TIME YOU TIED ME TO A TIRE!!

WHAT KIND OF ONIGIRI DO YOU WANT?!
I RECOMMEND THE ONES WITH VARIOUS YUMMY FILLINGS!
SHAMIKO, THOU WISHEST TO RUN A TRAINING CAMP.
THY TAIL REVEALS THY EXCITEMENT, CHILD!

AN ESSAY ON EMBARRASSMENT

LET'S START HERE: "MY DREAMS FOR THE FUTURE"!!
MAN, ESSAYS ARE SUCH A PAIN.
WHY SHOULD WE TELL THE TEACHER THIS STUFF?

WHAT DO YOU WANT TO DO, MOMO?
"NOTHING IN PARTICULAR."
NO WAY!

"I WANT TO BECOME AN AMAZING DARK MAGICAL GIRL."
COME ON, WRITE THAT.
YOU'RE LEFT-HANDED?
OVER MY DEAD BODY.
GRR!
GRR!
GRR!

HOW COME?!
BECAUSE I'LL LOOK BACK ON IT AS AN ADULT AND DIE OF SHAME.
?

A DEMON WHO CARES ABOUT SPECIAL DAYS

OKAY, MOVING ON! SUMMER JOURNAL!
I THOUGHT THE JOURNAL WAS OPTIONAL.
WELL, I DID IT. YOU CAN JUST INCLUDE THE HIGHLIGHTS.
PICTURE DIARY

LIKE, DID SOMETHING HAPPEN ON AUGUST X?
……
"I WOKE UP, ATE, WORKED OUT, AND WENT TO BED. THAT'S IT."
CACKLE
CACKLE
CACKLE

WHAAAAAT?! YOU LIAR!!
THAT'S THE DAY YOU FELL INTO DARKNESS!! YOU CAME TO FIND ME!!
AUGUST X IS YOUR "DARKNESS ANNIVERSARY"!!
YOU'RE BEING SUCH A PAIN, SHAMIKO!
I got lost in my own memories and my mortal enemy fell into darkness to save me.

NO FIGHTING IN THE HOUSE!
WE'RE VERY SORRY.

THANK GOODNESS FOR PART-TIME JOBS

I GUESS I COULD WRITE ABOUT HOW CATS ARE CUTE.
SOME MAGICAL GIRL. SHE'S FOOLING AROUND ON HER PHONE.
AH...

THE TAMA SAKURA-CHAN MANJU I GOT FROM THE BOSS!
MAYBE SOME SUGAR WOULD HELP HER BRAIN.
TAMA SAKURA MANJU
FLUTTER

!!
OH, RIGHT!!
TAMA ZOO

MO-MOOO!
IF YOU FINISH YOUR HOME-WORK THIS WEEK ...
I'LL GIVE YOU A PRIZE!

A DEMON WHO KNOWS HOW TO MOTIVATE HER VASSALS

TICKETS TO THE ZOO?
YES! AND THEY'RE LIMITED-EDITION VIP TICKETS, TOO.
THEY WERE A GIFT FROM MY BOSS ...
AND THEY'RE GOOD FOR SEVEN MORE DAYS.

I BET THE ZOO'S SUPER CROWDED RIGHT NOW.
BESIDES, I CAN'T LET GREED MOTIVATE ME.
GRR... THAT'S TRUE.
SHE'S FLOPPING AROUND IN MY HOUSE!
FLOOOP

ANYWAAAAY...
WHAT EXACTLY MAKES THEM VIP TICKETS?
LET ME SEE.
LOOKS LIKE RIGHT NOW, THEY GET YOU IN TO PET A BABY TIGER.

THE DEADLINE'S IN A WEEK, YOU SAID?
AH! YOU'RE SITTING UP!!
SO, FELINES ARE YOUR WEAK-NESS!!
FWSH!

WHAT MOMO WANTS TO DO

THANK GOOD-NESS! MOMO'S FINALLY WORK-ING!
SCORE ONE FOR THE DEMON SIDE!
HEY, SHAMIKO.

FOR THE ESSAY ...
I CAN'T THINK OF ANY BIG DREAMS OR PLANS FOR THE FUTURE...
BUT THERE IS ONE THING I'D LIKE RIGHT NOW.

I WANT TO EAT A BENTO THAT YOU'VE MADE FOR ME.
OUT-SIDE.
......!!

WATCH OUT! I'LL MAKE SO MUCH FOOD YOU CAN'T EAT IT ALL!
I'LL GET MY HOMEWORK DONE, TOO! LET'S ALL GO TOGETHER! TO THE ZOO!!

A HANDY FORM THAT DOESN'T NEED SLEEP

"Apparently, I was an orphan.

"My sister took me along with her a lot."

I GUESS IT'S BEEN TOUGH FOR MOMO, TOO.

I CAN'T REPLACE SAKURA-SAN.
BUT IF I TAKE MOMO TO LOTS OF PLACES...
THEN MAYBE ...

....
SKRTCH
SKRTCH
SKRTCH
SKRTCH

WHAT'S THAT SUP-POSED TO BE?
TRANS-FORMA-TION LITE?
WHAT A WEIRD GETUP.
IT HELPS ME FOCUS!

RETURN OF THE DARK MAGICAL GIRL

AT THIS RATE, I WON'T BE DONE IN TIME.
I'LL STILL MAKE YOU LUNCH, BUT YOU'LL HAVE TO GO TO THE ZOO WITHOUT ME.
WHAT?

WHAT ARE YOU SAYING?
ISN'T GOING WITH FRIENDS THE WHOLE POINT OF THE ZOO?
I SEEM TO REMEMBER YOU SMUGLY SAYING...
SOMETHING ABOUT "KEEPING YOUR PROMISES."
SHOOM...

WHY DID YOU TRANSFORM?! I'M SCARED!!
WE'RE NOT SLEEPING TONIGHT. THAT HOMEWORK'S GETTING DONE!
WAAAAAAAH!!

KEEP WORKING IN YOUR SLEEP!
DON'T THINK THIS MEANS... ZZZZ...

DON'T GIVE UP, SHAMIKO! BECOME A DEMON WHO CAN SOLVE PROBLEMS STEP-BY-STEP!!

"A" FOR EFFORT

A FEW DAYS LATER.
SHAMIKO!!
LOOK! I FINISHED IT IN THREE DAYS!

UUGH... NNGH...
HMM ...?
WORLD HISTORY WORKSHEET PACKET
MATH I-A
SLUMP...

WHAT'S GOING ON?
I'M GETTING SOME DÉJÀ VU HERE.
THE MATH PROBLEMS... I'M NOT DONE YET!

I TRIED SUPER-SERIOUSLY, AND I JUST COULDN'T DO THEM!!
I DON'T HAVE THE SKILLS!
THAT'S THE WORST POSSIBLE USE OF YOUR TIME.
MATH I-A

I MADE PLANS TO GO TO THE ZOO WITH MOMO AND MIKAN-SAN.
"I want to eat a bento that you've made for me."
THIS IS MY CHANCE TO SHOW WHAT A DEPEND-ABLE DEMON I AM.

HMM...
HRMMM...

I'LL CREATE THE MOST POWER-FUL BENTO EVER!
FIRST, A TEST RUN WITH WHAT I HAVE AT HOME!!
BWAA HA HA HA! BWAA HA HA... KOFF! KOFF!

SWF
WHAT DO YOU THINK OF THIS BENTO?
TO WHOM ART THOU SPEAK-ING, SHA-MIKO?

DON'TCHA WORRY--IT'S NATURAL!

HOW TO MAKE BENTO?
PLEASE SHOW ME HOW TO MAKE A BENTO THAT MAGICAL GIRLS WILL REALLY WANT TO EAT.

THE ONES WE SOLD THE OTHER DAY LOOKED REALLY NICE, SO...
AWW, YOU'RE SUCH A DEAR~!
SURE, I'LL TEACH YA! ♪

FIRST, CHOOSE YOUR INGREDIENTS!
WAIT... LEAVES?

FROM THE RIGHT...
WE'VE GOT PARALYSIS, SLEEP, AND FEVER-INDUCING, RIGHT THERE.
UM, I'M NOT TRYING TO DRUG THEM!

PANTONE BROWN

THE COLOR SCHEME IS PRETTY DULL.
I'D LIKE IT TO BE A BIT BRIGHTER FOR OUR OUTING.

WHY NOT MAKE IT DARKER?
THOU ART A DEMON, AFTER ALL.
BUT I'VE GOT TO IMPRESS THE MAGICAL GIRLS WITH THIS!

DEMON LUNCH: ENJOY THE SPLATTER!
CURSED
THEN WHY NOT COVER IT ALL WITH BLACK SEAWEED?
AND BLAST SOME KETCHUP IN THE MIDDLE!
THAT'S NOT WHAT I MEANT BY "IMPRESS"!!

WOW, SHAMIKO, YOUR BENTO LOOKS LIKE DEAD LEAVES!
LET'S FORGET ABOUT THE WHOLE VASSAL THING.
I DON'T HAVE ENOUGH BENTO-MAKING SKILLS!!
I NEED HELP.

LICO-KUN CAN'T TAKE A HINT

YOU WANT YOUR SIDE DISHES TO HAVE DIFFERENT COLORS AND FLAVORS.
SWEET, SOUR, AND SALTY ARE THE BASICS.

AND IF YOU USE RED, YELLOW, GREEN, WHITE, AND BLACK, IT'LL LOOK TASTY.
LET'S GIVE IT A TRY, SHALL WE?
WOW, LICO-SAN, YOU CAN MAKE ANYTHING!

WELL, SURE. I'VE LIVED ALL OVER THE PLACE ...
SO I'VE LEARNED ALL KINDS OF COOKIN'.
BUT Y'KNOW, NO MATTER WHERE I GO...

I ALWAYS END UP GETTING CHASED AWAY. I WONDER WHY.
?
YOU REALLY DON'T KNOW?!
IT'S BECAUSE YOU SHOULDN'T DRUG YOUR BOSSES!

PUT YOUR FEELINGS INTO IT

SO, IF IT'S A COLORFUL BENTO YA WANT...
I RATHER LIKE LEAF COLORS, MYSELF.
BUT THE KEY IS TO PUT YOUR FEELINGS INTO IT.

SPA-SPARKLE
SPARKLE
FIRST, PUT THE FEELING OF "ENJOY EATING THIS" INTO YOUR PALMS.
UH, WHY ARE YOUR HANDS GLOWING?
ARE YOU ALL RIGHT?
SPARKLE
SPARKLE

C'MERE, BOSS~! EAT THIIIS!
UH... NO THANK YOU.
JUST EAT IIIIT!
SCOOT...

L-LICO-KUN, I CAN FEEL RAINBOW LEAVES FLOATING IN MY STOMACH!
NOW, AIN'T THAT NIIICE!
I'M SORRY, PLEASE TEACH ME SOMETHING ELSE!

YES, A LITTLE

BUT I WANNA SHOW YOU PRETTY THINGS 'CAUSE I LOVE YA SO MUCH, BOSS!
SWP
I FORGIVE YOU!
WOW, THAT WAS FAST!

I S'POSE I GOT CAUGHT BY MIKO-HAN AND CHASED OUT A FEW TIMES, TOO.
I'VE BEEN INTERESTED IN COOKING SINCE I FIRST TRANSFORMED, Y'SEE.

I SNUCK INTO LOTS OF KITCHENS ...
AND DID MY DARNDEST TO COOK GOOD THINGS.
BUT WHEN I WAS A LI'L FOX, SOMETIMES I USED A TAD *TOO MUCH* FEELING...

AND MAYBE I CAUSED AN ITTY-BITTY RUCKUS OR TWO?
FOOOOD! FOOOD!
CLOSED TODAY
ARE YOU SURE IT WAS *JUST* "ITTY-BITTY"?

THE BOSS CONTEMPLATES THE MEANING OF LOVE

SO ...
WHEN THE MIKO GALS FOUND ME, I KEPT MOVING, AND I ENDED UP HERE.
GOSH, I HAD NO IDEA!

I REGRET IT NOW, THOUGH.
A NATURAL SMILE IS THE BEST REPAYMENT FOR MY COOKING.

I'M REAL HAPPY THAT I GET TO COOK IN THIS TOWN.
IT'S ALL THANKS TO SAKURA-HAN AND THE BOSS.
LICO-KUN!!

I GET MEALS AND A PLACE TO SLEEP... I DON'T HAFTA LEAVE THE KITCHEN IF I DON'T FEEL LIKE IT...
AND LATELY, I HAVEN'T EVEN DEALT WITH CUSTOMERS! I'M SO HAPPY!
LICO-KUN?

DEMON IN DISTRESS

WELL... THE MIKO-HAN AREN'T QUITE SO PUSHY THESE DAYS...
BUT STILL, WATCH YOUR BACK.
WHAT EXACTLY IS A MAGICAL GIRL, ANYWAY?

DOES SOME-ONE MAKE THEM FIGHT?
DO THEY GET RE-WARDS FOR BEATING DEMONS AND STUFF?
THEY'RE HUMAN GIRLS WHO MAKE CONTRACTS WITH THE "LIGHT CLAN"... OR SO I HEAR.

THEY'RE CHOSEN BY "LIGHT CLAN MESSENGERS" WHO POSSESS LIVING THINGS.
WHAT THE HECK IS THE LIGHT CLAN?!

BEATS ME.
AAARGH.

THE PERKS OF BEING A MAGICAL GIRL, REVEALED!

WE'VE NEVER REALLY TALKED MUCH WITH THE MAGICAL GIRLS.
PERHAPS YOU SHOULD ASK MOMO-DONO.

REGARDING REWARDS, HOWEVER ...
WHEN A MAGICAL GIRL WEAKENS AND IMMOBILIZES ONE OF US...
SHE GETS A "TOKEN OF VICTORY" FROM THE MESSEN-GERS.

I'VE HEARD THE GIRLS GET A REWARD IF THEY COLLECT LOTS OF TOKENS.
"TOKENS," HUH...?

THE MORE THEY GATHER, THE BIGGER THE WISH THEY CAN HAVE GRANTED.
......!!

LIKO'S DIALECT IS RUBBING OFF ON SHAMIKO

THEY CAN GET WISHES GRANTED?!
THAT...THAT SOUNDS GREAT!
YES, WE'RE BASICALLY WALKING POWER-UPS.

BUT MANY MAGICAL GIRLS ARE GENTLER THESE DAYS.
SO YOU'RE SAFE AS LONG AS YOU PLAY BY THE LOCAL RULES... USUALLY.
MOMO AND MIKAN-SAN ARE PROTECTING ME...
EVEN THOUGH I'M A POWER-UP!

I-I HAVE TO MAKE A SUPER-YUMMY BENTO...
ONE THAT WILL MAKE THE MAGICAL GIRLS SMILE!!
NOW THAT'S THE SPIRIT~!

HERE'S A MUSHROOM THAT'LL KEEP 'EM SMIIILIN'!
THAT AIN'T RIGHT!!

HELPFUL FOR WHEN YOU FORGET A PEN

THE MEAT'S ALL PREPARED. TIME TO GET COOKIN'!
ONLY ONE OF THE WOKS IS SEASONED, SO I'LL TAKE CARE OF T'OTHER.
OH, IT'S OKAY! I THINK I CAN MAKE A PAN.
SNAP

"MAKE" ONE?
THIS IS A STAFF I INHERITED FROM MY DAD.
I CAN TURN IT INTO ALL KINDS OF THINGS!

WHY, IT'S A PERFECTLY SEASONED WOK!
THE OIL'S JUST RIGHT!
THAT'S INCREDIBLE! IT COMPLETELY SKIPPED ALL THE STEPS!

YUP! PRETTY HANDY, RIIIGHT?
"HANDY" DOESN'T EVEN BEGIN TO DESCRIBE THIS!

THE POOREST DEMON IN THE METRO TOKYO AREA

ARE THERE ANY RULES FOR ITS TRANS-FORMA-TIONS?
AS LONG AS IT'S SOMETHING "POLE-SHAPED" ...
THERE DON'T SEEM TO BE A LOT OF LIMITS.

SAY, COULD I HAVE THAT, HUN?
UM, I DON'T THINK SO--
LICO-KUN, YOU'VE GOT TO WORK ON YOUR IMPULSE CONTROL !!

YOU CAN ENTER PEOPLE'S DREAMS TOO, RIGHT?
AS LONG AS THEY'RE ASLEEP, THEN USUALLY, YES.

SHOULD YOU REALLY BE WORKING IN SOME DINKY CAFÉ?
YOU PROMISE YOU WON'T GET BORED AND QUIT?
HUH? WHAT? PLEASE LET ME KEEP WORKING HERE!

THE OIL WAS TOO HOT, HUN

IF YOU FELT SO INCLINED ...
YOU MIGHT BE ABLE TO HELP A LOT OF PEOPLE.

WHEN ONE HAS GREAT POTENTIAL, STILL IN ITS INFANCY...
THERE ARE MANY DIRECTIONS ONE'S FUTURE COULD TAKE, GOOD AND BAD.

SHE SHOULD BE FINE, AS LONG AS A STRICT MAGICAL GIRL DOESN'T FIND HER.

THE CHICKEN BURNED TO A CRISP IN SECONDS!
I GUESS EVEN AN ALL-PURPOSE STAFF NEEDS HEAT CONTROL.
THEN AGAIN, WELL... HMM.

SAY...

I FINISHED SOME TEST SIDE DISHES!
AIN'T THAT NIIICE!

SAY! WHY DON'TCHA PACK IT ALL IN THIS?
A NICE BENTO DE-SERVES A NICE FANCY BOX~!
THANKS, THAT WOULD BE GREAT!

HERE'S THE THING, THOUGH.
THIS BOX IS MEANT FOR FOUR OR FIVE PEOPLE.
YOU'RE GOING WITH TWO MAGICAL-GIRL-HANS, RIGHT? THAT'LL BE A BIT TOO MUUUCH!

SAY, NOW...
UH-OH.

TOURING ALL THE CUTE ANIMALS-- INCLUDING MAGICAL GIRLS

MOMO!! MIKAN-SAN! GOOD MORNING!
HEY, SHAMIKO.

HOWDY THERE, MOMO-HAN~!
UM... HELLO THERE...
YOU'RE TOO HEAVY!
WHAT?

I'M SO SORRY...
I COULDN'T STOP HER.
IT'S MY FIRST TIME SEEING A ZOO! THIS'LL BE A REAL TREAT!
THANKS FOR HAVING ME, DEARIES~!

MOMO-HAN, THAT'S AN AWFUL CUTE OUTFIT YOU'RE WEARIN'!
HOW COME? HOW COME, HUH?
UH, YEAH, I'M GONNA GO CHANGE.
DON'T GIVE UP, SHAMIKO! TIME TO GET SOCIAL AT THE ZOO!!

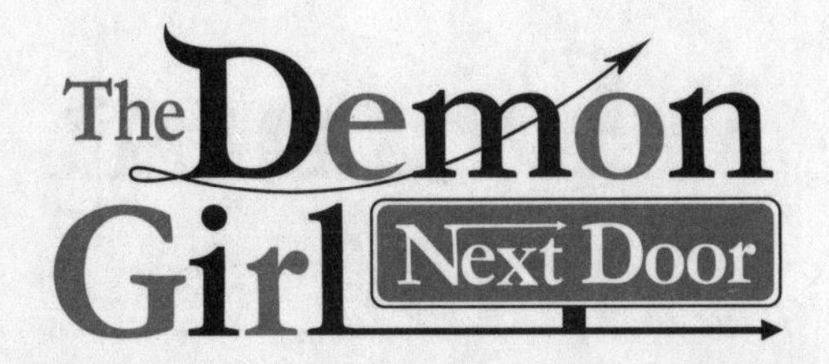
The Demon Girl Next Door

The Demon
Girl
Next Door

DEMON
Very weak at the moment, but hopefully that will change.

The story so far:
It's a fun day at the zoo!!
ALL RIGHT, LET'S HAVE A BLAST TODAY!

THAT ISN'T THE PROBLEM, YUKO-KUN.
IT'S JUST ...
I'M SENSING SOME STORM CLOUDS NEARBY, YOU SEE...
SHAKE
SHAKE
SHAKE

ARE YOU SURE ...
IT'S ALL RIGHT THAT WE CAME ALONG?
OF COURSE! THIS TICKET ADMITS UP TO FIVE PEOPLE.
TAMA ZOO
TICKETS
ADMISSION

WHAT ARE YOU DOING HERE?
REAL!
The story so far:
It was supposed to be a fun day at the zoo.

A PINK HEART'S DAM ON THE VERGE OF BURSTING

WE'RE ON A MISSION OF PURE FRIENDSHIP, MOMO-HAN!
WHY, YOU'RE BEING DOWNRIGHT MEEEAN!
YOU EVEN CHANGED OUT OF YOUR CUTE LI'L GETUP!

MAKE IT QUICK.
Translation: Explain yourself before the dam in my heart bursts.

MOMO-HAN, YA LIKE CRITTERS, RIGHT?
WELL, ME AND THE BOSS HERE ARE CRITTERS, TOO!
SO, I FIGURED YOU'D BE PLEASED AS PUNCH TO HAVE US ALONG!
AIN'T THAT THOUGHTFUL?

I SEE.
Translation: I'm not going to get a clear answer, so I'll stop trying.

LET'S ENJOY IT TOGETHER!

LICO-KUN, THAT'S NOT IT AT ALL!
OUR GOAL IS FAR MORE IMPORTANT!!
WE'RE GETTING THE MAGICAL GIRLS TO--
GAAAAAH!!

GU...GWUHH...
AH-AH-AH!
BOSS?!
MY NEARLY-HEALED BACK...

SORRY I'M SO FRAIL... GO ON AND ENJOY THE ZOO WITHOUT ME!
YOU'RE RIGHT. LICO-SAN SHOULD TAKE YOU HOME AND--

WE COULD NEVER DO THAT TO YOU!!
I'LL CARRY YOUR THINGS!!
WAIT, WE'RE REALLY DOING THIS?

WAY BETTER THAN HUMAN EARS, Y'HEAR~?

I'M GLAD THE AIR'S CLEARED A BIT.
I'M SORRY...SO SORRY...
SAY, MOMO ...

WOULD YOU HAVE PREFERRED IT TO BE JUST US TWO, AFTER ALL?
WITH SHAMIKO?
HUH?!
NO, NO... IF WE CAN ALL HAVE FUN TOGETHER, THAT'S GREAT.

BUT I PRACTI-CALLY ATTACKED THOSE TWO WHEN WE FIRST MET...
SO I'M AFRAID LICO-SAN MIGHT NOT LIKE ME MUCH.

AW, THAT AIN'T TRUE AT AAALL!
I THINK YOU'RE CUTE AS A BUTTON, HUN~!
SHE HAS ANIMAL-LEVEL HEARING!!

DIFFERENT SENSIBILITIES

ALL RIGHT, LET'S GOOO!
WE BROUGHT LOTSA FOOD...
SO THOSE TUMMIES BETTER GET GROWLIN'!

BABY MALAYAN TAPIRS HAVE SUCH INTRICATE PATTERNS ON THEIR FUR!
YOU'RE RIGHT! SO DIFFERENT FROM THE ADULTS.
JAPANESE FIELD MOUSE
......

YA LIKE TEENSY LITTLE CRITTERS, EH?
I GUESS ...
SO DO I!

THEY COOK THROUGH NICE AN' EASY...
SO YOU CAN BOIL 'EM, GRILL 'EM, OR FRY 'EM UP!
WE STILL DON'T SEE EYE TO EYE, DO WE?

I'M NOT A BAD TAPIR!

IT'S QUITE LIVELY HERE DURING SUMMER BREAK.
I WONDER WHAT THAT CROWD'S DOING?

BOSS?!
OH, UM, I'M NOT PART OF THE PETTING ZOO.
NOT THAT I MIND, BUT...

PHOTOS ARE 1,800 YEN A POP!
LICO-KUN, DON'T EXPLOIT THESE NICE PEOPLE!

I HEARD THERE'S A TAPIR ON THE LOOSE!
AH! NO, I'M A FREE-RANGE TAPIR!
FREE-RANGE?

THE BOSS'S CONCERNS

I'M SORRY FOR THROWING A WRENCH IN YOUR GIRLS' DAY OUT.
IT WAS NOTHING! OH, BUT...

WHAT WAS THAT "IMPORTANT GOAL" YOU MENTIONED?
!
AHH, THAT'S RIGHT!

WE HAVE DIFFERENT SENSES FROM YOU HUMANS...
SO SOMETIMES WE PICK UP ON UNUSUAL THINGS YOU MIGHT NOT NOTICE.

AND, WELL, I'M CONCERNED ABOUT MOMO-DONO.
WHAT DO YOU MEAN?

ESCAPED PARTY MEMBERS

MOMO!!
I FINALLY FOUND YOU!
SORRY, I GOT FIXATED ON THE ANIMALS AND FELL BEHIND.

UM, SO...
EVERYONE ELSE ACTUALLY HAD TO GO HOME.
HUH?

I've got to water my citrus plants.
Uh-oh, I think I left the fryer on.
Gahh!! My chronic sleepiness!!
OR SO THEY SAID.
WHAT ON EARTH?

AFTER WE MADE ALL THAT FOOD, TOO.
OH, JEEZ ...
WERE THEY TRYING TO BE POLITE?

DEMON DEBRIEFING

I'M SORRY EVERYTHING GOT SO OUT OF HAND.
HUH? NO, NO...
ALL THE CRAZINESS WAS ACTUALLY KIND OF FUN.

I'M GLAD TO HEAR IT!!
ANYWAY, THIS SEEMS LIKE A GOOD TIME FOR LUNCH!

SO, UM! I... WANT TO BE CLOSER TO YOU, MOMO.
NOW THAT WE'VE GOT THIS TIME...
WE CAN FINALLY HAVE A NICE LONG TALK.

WHAT ARE YOUR DREAMS?
WHY DID YOU BECOME A MAGICAL GIRL?
YOUR WEAKNESSES?
YOUR LEAST FAVORITE FOODS?
THAT'S QUITE THE BARRAGE OF QUESTIONS, HUH?!
JAB
JAB

FRESH PEACH LEG-SWEEP THROW

I REALLY LOVE THIS TOWN...
SO I WANT TO KNOW MORE ABOUT THE ONE WHO'S PROTECTING IT WITH ME.

I FEEL THE SAME WAY.
BUT...
GRAB
HUH?

YOUR APPROACH...
IS MESSED UP!!
SMACK!
YEEK!
FLIP

I DO DECLAAARE!
COULDN'T YA JUST PLAY ALONG?
I KNEW YOU WERE UP TO NO GOOD...
LICO-SAN!
FWOO OO OOOOSH...

NOT A DEMONIC TONE

SO, IF I'D FALLEN FOR THAT, I WOULD'VE EATEN YOUR MAGIC HERBS!
HOW DID YA KNOW?

EVERYTHING WAS ALL WRONG!
WHOO-EEEE! THIS GIRL!
YOUR TONE, MANNERISMS, EYES, BREATHING PATTERNS, TAIL MOVEMENT, AND POSTURE!
AND MOST OF ALL...

SHAMIKO WOULD *NEVER* BE THAT STRAIGHTFORWARD WITH ME!
GOTCHA! WELL, THANKS FOR ALL THE TIPS!

LICO-KUN! MOMO-DONO! THERE YOU ARE!!
BOOOOSS!
SHE SAW RIGHT THROUGH MY *PRAAANK*!

HEALTHY AND FLAVORFUL COOKING

I CAN'T TAKE MY EYES OFF HER FOR A SECOND!
I'M SORRY ABOUT LICO-KUN!
TAPIR!
A TAPIIIR!
AH, PLEASE GET UP.
THERE ARE CHILDREN WATCHING.

IF YOU WANT MOMO-DONO TO TAKE MEDICINE...
YOU SHOULD JUST ASK HER DIRECTLY!
"MEDICINE"?

MOMO-HAN... YOUR MAGIC'S BEEN AWFUL UNSTABLE LATELY.
THAT'S WHY I WANTED YOU TO EAT MY COOKING.
THIS DISH IS REAL GOOD FOR CALMING THE SPIRIT.

WHAT *COOKING*? THIS IS A PILE OF RAW LEAVES.
I FIGURED, WITH A LITTLE TRANSFORMATION, YOU'D EAT 'EM RIGHT UP.

HONEST LICO-KUN

MOMO-DONO USED EXTREME METHODS WHEN SHE FELL INTO DARKNESS.
TAKING STRANGE DRUGS, CHANGING BACK HER ATTRIBUTES BY FORCE...
ALL OF THAT MIGHT HAVE TAKEN A TOLL ON HER CORE.

IT'S BAD FOR BODY AND MIND ALIKE TO LET THAT SORTA THING FESTER...
BUT YOU WERE SO WARY OF US, WE COULDN'T JUST OFFER.

SO, YOU TRANSFORMED TO TRY TO FEED ME MEDICINE?
LICO-KUN MEANS WELL, REALLY.

WELL, I CAN'T SAY I WASN'T A TEENSY BIT EXCITED TO TRICK A MIKO-HAN INTO EATIN' LEAVES.
THAT'S ENOUGH OUT OF YOU!!

FORGOTTEN GOAL (SEE TWO CHAPTERS AGO)

THAT REMINDS ME... WHAT ABOUT YOUR OTHER GOAL, MOMO?

THE VIP TICKET PERK...

WHERE YOU GET TO PET A BABY TIGER?

FREEZE...

......
VIP EXCLUSIVE PETTING ZOO SESSION ENDED AT 2 PM.
CLOSED
I... COMPLETELY FORGOT!

I'M REAL FLUFFY WHEN I TURN BACK INTO A FOX.
YOU CAN HOLD ME, Y'HEAR?
SNAP
NO THANK YOU!

DON'T THINK THIS MEANS...
YOU'VE WON.
MOMO, LET ME HOLD HER NEXT!
DON'T GIVE UP, SHAMIKO! ALL ILL FEELINGS WILL BE FORGOTTEN AROUND THE DINING TABLE!!

THE KIND THAT BUFFALO EAT

W-WELL... LET'S ALL MAKE UP AND EAT LUNCH, SHALL WE?!
YEAH, WE MADE A TON OF FOOD.

I *DID* MEAN IT WHEN I SAID I WANTED TO BE CLOSER TO YOU, HONEST.
IF YOU'D JUST EXPLAINED YOURSELF, I WOULD'VE EATEN THE HERBS.

YA MEAN IT?
THEN EAT EIGHT HUNDRED OF THESE BEFORE LUNCH!
FWUMP
I GUESS WE STILL DON'T SEE EYE TO EYE, AFTER ALL.

YOU SAID YOU'D EAT 'EM!
YES, BUT THERE'S A LIMIT!
I CAME TO EAT BENTO FOOD, NOT LEAVES!
COME ON, DON'T FIGHT!

SECONDS!!
DEMON GIRL NEXT DOOR
(CHAPTER 40)
~ LICO-KUN'S YUKATA SURPRISE ~

HERE'S YOUR YUKATA. THANKS AGAIN.
OH, I DIDN'T NEED THAT OLD THING BACK!

IT'S JUST A LEAF, Y'KNOW.
HUH?
PRESTO !!

SEE?! IT'S AN ILLUSION !!
JUST A LITTLE FOX SPIRIT SECRET MOVE~!
......
WHOO OO OOSH

SO...
I WAS WALKING AROUND WEARING NOTHING BUT A LEAF?!
SHUDDER...

DID YOU NAME THEM?
AKAMI AND SHIROMI.
THAT SOUNDS MORE LIKE SASHIMI* THAN PETS.

* Akami and shiromi are both, in fact, types of fish used in sushi and sashimi.

SECONDS!!
DEMON GIRL NEXT DOOR
(CHAPTER 43)
~ TRAGEDY ON TWO LEGS ~

THE BOSS HURTS HIMSELF A LOT.
ARE YOU ALL RIGHT?
YES. I'M SORRY... MY MEDICINAL PATCH IS KICKING IN, SO I'M FINE NOW.

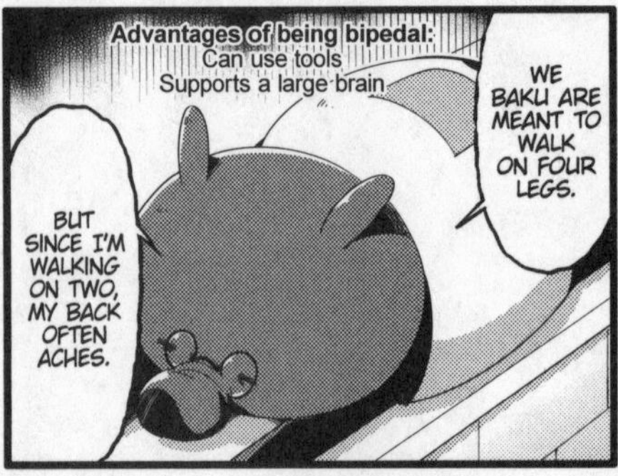
Advantages of being bipedal:
Can use tools
Supports a large brain
WE BAKU ARE MEANT TO WALK ON FOUR LEGS.
BUT SINCE I'M WALKING ON TWO, MY BACK OFTEN ACHES.

OH NO...THAT MUST BE HARD!
IT'S HELLISH! BUT YOU SEE...
IF I WANT TO FIT INTO HUMAN SOCIETY...
I HAVE TO WALK ON TWO LEGS.

I'D THINK AN ANIMAL WALKING ON TWO LEGS WOULD ACTUALLY STAND OUT MORE.
BUT...I GUESS IT DOESN'T MATTER.
HOW AWFUL!

Boss's Three-Stage Groveling Technique
Grovel.

Sliding Grovel.
Yoga Grovel.

THAT DAY, CHIYODA MOMO WOKE UP FEELING... OFF.
BEEP BEEP
BEEP BEEP
CRACK!!
MORNING, METAKO.
HUNH, YOU SOUND WEIRD.
VRROWWWR!
MRROW!
WRROW!
HUH?
THE GLASS BROKE?
FLAASH
?!
......
WHAT THE ...?!
HER RECENTLY ACQUIRED MODE!
THAT'S RIGHT!! THIS IS...
MAGICAL GIRL CHIYODA MOMO'S DARKNESS FORM!!

FIRST THINGS FIRST

RATTLE
M-MOMO, ARE YOU OKAY?!
I HEARD A WEIRD NOISE AND SAW A FLASH ALL THE WAY FROM MY ROOM!!
UH... SHAMIKO?

LOOKS LIKE...
I'VE KINDA FALLEN BACK INTO DARKNESS.

......
WHY?
I'M NOT SURE.
AND I CAN'T CHANGE BACK, EITHER.

OKAY, THIS IS HUGE!
WH-WHAAAT...?!
BUT FIRST, CAN I TOUCH YOUR ABS?!
CAN'T THAT WAIT?!

PEACH HOST BODY PRODUCTION

HOW DO YOU FEEL?
WELL, I'M NOT TIRED OR SORE...
BUT I CAN'T CONTROL MY BODY WITH MAGIC LIKE USUAL.

CRRRUNCH
SEE? I CAN'T REGULATE MY STRENGTH.
IT'S JUST ON, FULL-THROTTLE.
I BET SHE COULD DO THAT NORMALLY.

AT THIS RATE, I'LL USE UP ALL MY MAGIC AND REVERT TO CORE MODE.
......!!
SO...I'VE GOT TO CHANGE BACK RIGHT AWAY.

ART THOU LEAVING US TODAY, MOMO?!
HOW SAD! PLEASE MAKE LOTS OF HOST BODIES BEFORE THOU GOEST!
WANT TO SEE IF I CAN CRUSH YOUR REAL BODY, LILITH-SAN?

EARLY MORNING WAKE-UP PRANK, MIKAN VERSION

GOOD MORNING, MIKAN!!
MWUH?!
JOLT
Unruly Oranges FREE STYLE

HUH? WHAT?
WHY THE ODD GETUP?
HIT MY CORE HARD WITHOUT KILLING ME.
WHAT?!

NO TIME TO EX-PLAIN! JUST TRANS-FORM!!
OUT-SIDE! NOW!
WHAAA...
SERI-OUSLY, WHAT IS THIS?!
I'M SORRY! I'M SORRY! I'M SO SORRY!

BAM BAM BAM
WHAT A WAY TO...
WAKE ME UUUP!!
KA-BLAM

STYLISH ENTRANCE

MAYBE I'LL TURN BACK IF MIKAN HITS ME WITH MAGIC AGAIN.
LET'S GO.
OH... YEAH, MAYBE.
BUT I DON'T THINK THAT SHOULD HAPPEN TOO OFTEN.

IS SOME-THING BOTHER-ING YOU?
UM... WELL...IT'S LIKE MY BOSS SAID YESTERDAY.
YOU PUSHED YOURSELF TOO HARD WHEN YOU FELL INTO DARKNESS.

IF I HADN'T DONE THAT, I WOULD FEEL MUCH WORSE THAN I DO NOW.
I DON'T REGRET THAT CHOICE...
SO PLEASE DON'T WORRY ABOUT IT.
ALL... ALL RIGHT.

LET'S JUST STAY CALM AND GIVE IT OUR BEST SHOT!
KA-
THAT DOESN'T MEAN BREAK DOWN THE DOOR!
I TOLD YOU, I CAN'T CONTROL MY STRENGTH!
BOOM!

MOMO BECOMES ARROW PEACH (SECOND TIME IN FIVE CHAPTERS)

DID IT WORK?
NO GOOD. I STILL CAN'T TURN BACK.

I BELIEVE I HIT YOU AS BEST I COULD.
SHOO
BUT, REALLY...
OOM

I DON'T APPRECIATE BEING WOKEN UP AND HAVING TO SHOOT MY FRIEND FULL OF MAGIC ARROWS!!
THINK OF A GIRL'S FEELINGS!!
スカッ
SSHHWr
I REALLY AM SORRY.
HMPH, IT'S FINE!!

WHAT ABOUT MY FEELINGS? I WAS STRUCK BY MIKAN'S CURSE.
THOU OUGHTEST TO THINK OF ME, TOO.
ANCESTOR, HOW'D YOU GET UP THERE?

LICO-KUN LEARNED "CONSIDERATION"!

SHAMIKO, CAN YOU CONTACT CAFÉ ASURA?

OH DEAR. AIN'T THAT A PIIICKLE!
MY MEDICINE TAKES A SMIDGE OF TIME TO KICK IN.
MIGHT NOT HELP MUCH, AFTER THE FACT.

THE CALMING STUFF'S MORE TO PREVENT PROBLEMS THAN FIX 'EM, Y'HEEEAR!
AH, IS THAT SO?
YOU OKAY, HUN?

D-DON'T BE GLUM! IT WOULDA BEEN TOO LATE EVEN IF YOU'D EATEN IT SOONER!!
IT AIN'T YOUR FAULT, MOMO-HAN!!
SO, YOU CAN PASS ON WITHOUT ANY REGRETS!!
LICO-KUN, YOU'RE REALLY NOT HELPING!!

PEACH-COLORED COUNTDOWN

WHY NOT ASK OGURA SION?
SHE MAYETH BE ABLE TO HELP THEE.
HER NUMBER'S IN MY CELL PHONE, IN MY ROOM.

CRAAACKED!!
OH NO, IT'S BRO-KEN!

AAH...IT MUST'VE HAPPENED WHEN MY ALARM WENT OFF.
NOW WE CAN'T GET HER NUMBER!

M-MOMO?!
SWSH
UH-OH! I'M RUNNING LOW ON MAGIC.
SHH...
WHY'RE YOU TURNING SEE-THROUGH?!

MOST PEOPLE CALL THAT "STALKING"

WE'VE GOT TO GET AHOLD OF OGURA-SAN SOMEHOW!
OH GOSH, OH GOSH, WHAT DO I DO?
YOU RANG?

CREEEP...
O-OGURA-SAN?!
IT SEEMED LIKE YOU NEEDED ME, SO HERE I AM!
HOW DID YOU KNOW?

I HEARD IT ON THE MIC I INSTALLED IN YOUR EVIL STATUE.
ALSO, I PATROL YOUR NEIGHBOR-HOOD FIVE TIMES A WEEK.
......
KURARA

WELL, STILL, THANK YOU VERY MUCH!!
SHA-MIKO...
YOUR GRATITUDE HAS OVER-COME YOUR CAUTION!

THOU HAST INSTALLED A MICROPHONE WITHIN ME?

I'VE BEEN WORKED UP SINCE YOUR DREAM QUEST.
I DID LOTS OF RESEARCH, HOPING I COULD HELP!
EVEN SO, STALKING BEITH A CRIME.
DO YOU KNOW WHY I SUDDENLY WENT DARK AGAIN?
GLOOM

THIS IS JUST A HYPOTHESIS...
BUT I THINK YOUR NEGATIVE EMOTIONS MAY HAVE TRIGGERED IT.
NEGATIVE EMOTIONS?
YOU KNOW... LIKE JEALOUSY, PARANOIA, GREED.

LEGENDS SAY THAT LONG AGO, MEMBERS OF THE LIGHT CLAN WOULD FALL INTO DARKNESS...
WHEN THEY WERE CONSUMED WITH NEGATIVE THOUGHTS.
IN REALITY, IT WOULDN'T HAPPEN SO EASILY...

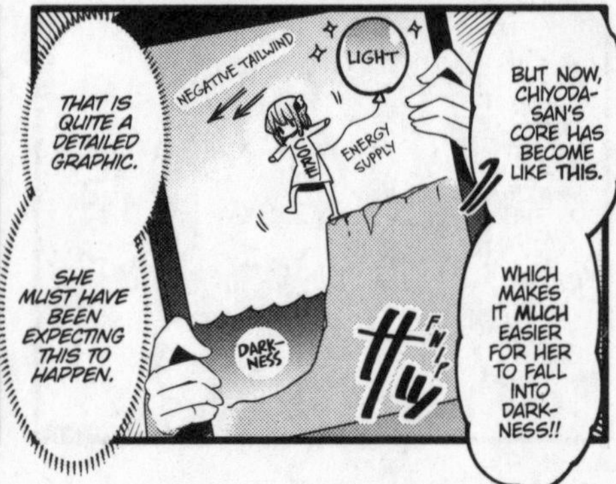
BUT NOW, CHIYODA-SAN'S CORE HAS BECOME LIKE THIS.
WHICH MAKES IT MUCH EASIER FOR HER TO FALL INTO DARKNESS!!
LIGHT
NEGATIVE TAILWIND
ENERGY SUPPLY
DARKNESS
THAT IS QUITE A DETAILED GRAPHIC.
SHE MUST HAVE BEEN EXPECTING THIS TO HAPPEN.

MOMO-CHAN WAVERS

YOUR CORE HAS SLIPPED INTO DARKNESS.
YOU'RE CUT OFF FROM THE LIGHT CLAN RIGHT NOW.
SO, HOW DO I TURN BACK?

BUT... IF YOU MAKE PEACE WITH YOUR RECENT NEGATIVE EMOTIONS...
YOUR LINK WILL BE RESTORED, AND YOU CAN TURN BACK!! MAYBE.
MEANING?

YOU'VE JUST GOT TO SPILL EVERY LITTLE DETAIL...
ABOUT ANYTHING THAT'S BOTHERED YOU LATELY!
KIRARA

IN THAT CASE, I DON'T NEED TO TURN BACK.
DON'T GIVE UP, DARN IT!!

PEACH PRIDE IS EASILY BRUISED

MOMO! PLEASE TELL US WHAT'S UPSET YOU LATELY!!
WELL, I DO HAVE A GUESS ...
BUT I DON'T WANT TO SAY IT HERE.

YOU SAID WE'D GIVE IT OUR BEST SHOT!!
LIFE IS ALL ABOUT SHARING THY SHAME!
IF YOU DISAPPEAR, I'LL CRY, DO YOU HEAR?!
......
YESTERDAY ...

I never got to eat Shamiko's bento lunch.
It was so hard to wait.
I was really looking forward to it.

THAT MADETH THEE FALL INTO DARKNESS?
THOU ART A CUTE ONE!
I'M A PETTY, PATHETIC LITTLE PERSON, ALL RIGHT?

RETRO BENTO FOOD HAS A LONG SHELF LIFE

I WANT TO VANISH FROM THIS WORLD ASAP.
MOMO'S IN BAD SHAPE, IN MORE WAYS THAN ONE! WE'D BETTER GIVE HER A BENTO, STAT!
R-RIGHT!
WOO-OO-OO-OOSH...

BUT MAKING A BENTO TAKES A LONG TIME!
MOMO'S MAGIC MIGHT RUN OUT WHILE I'M COOKING!!
WHAT SHOULD I MAKE? WHAT SHOULD I MAKE? AAAH!
SHAMIKO, DOST THOU NOT HAVE ONE AT THE READY?

THE VERY FIRST ONE THAT THOU MADEST.
THE DRY-LEAF BENTO!!

I...DON'T WANNA GIVE HER THIS...
BUT THERE IS NO TIME.
THOU MADEST THIS BENTO ON THY OWN! BE PROUD!

IT'S PLAIN BUT VERY NUTRITIOUS

IT'S A NICE, SHAMIKO-STYLE BENTO.
WHAT'S THAT SUPPOSED TO MEAN?! JUST EAT!!

CAN'T... I'LL BREAK THE CHOPSTICKS.
AARGH, FINE!! OPEN YOUR DARN MOOOUTH!!!

MUNCH MUNCH
WELL, MOMO? ARE YOU CONTENT?
UH-HUH...

ぽ
POO
ふ
OOF!

PEACH, LOADING UP ON KARMA

I TURNED BACK.
GREAT, IT WORKED!

THANK YOU, EVERYONE.
SORRY FOR THE TROUBLE.
YOU SHOULD NIP ANY NEW CHAOTIC FEELINGS IN THE BUD, THOUGH.
HUH?

YOU'LL PROBABLY BE VULNERABLE TO THE DARKNESS FOR A WHILE YET.
IF YOU HAPPEN TO FALL INTO DARKNESS AGAIN...
LET ME COLLECT MORE DATA, OKAY?

WAIT... THIS MIGHT KEEP HAPPENING?
DO YOUR BEST, MOMO-SAN! KEEP FIGHTING, EVEN IF YOUR MENTAL STATE IS A TICKING TIME BOMB!

MOMO SEEMS WORN OUT.
ARE YOU ALL RIGHT?
MY CORE IS IN ROUGH SHAPE.

CHI-YODA-SAN.
THERE'S A PLACE WHERE YOU CAN GET ALL BETTER ...
O-OGURA-SAN?!
スタッ
NWOOP...

I USED UP MOST OF ITS STRENGTH WHEN I FELL INTO DARK-NESS...
BUT IT SHOULD HEAL ONCE I GET SOME REST.
OH, IT WILL HEAL...

AND IT'S CALLED ...
"CHIYODA SAKURA'S SECRET SPRING"!
IT'S A HIDDEN SPRING THAT CAN RE-STORE MAGICAL GIRLS!!
FIRST, EXPLAIN WHAT YOU'RE DOING IN THE CEILING!

A ZERO-TO-SIXTY TYPE OF PERSON

WHY WAS I IN THE CEILING? BECAUSE THE CEILING WAS THERE!
THAT'S DEEP!
BUT...A SPRING THAT RESTORES MAGICAL GIRLS?

DEEP IN THE MOUNTAINS OF TAMA...
THERE'S A MIRACULOUS SPRING FUUULL OF MAGIC.
※ARTIST'S INTERPRETATION.
THEY SAY IT BEGAN AS A POOL OF PURE WATER, DEEP IN A CAVE.

LOOM
THEN A HOLE OPENED UP IN THE CAVE'S CEILING--
AND THE MOONLIGHT WENT FLAAASH!!
AND THE MAGIC WENT BLOOOSH!!
EEK!

THE NEGATIVE IONS WENT PWAA-AH!
AND THE NATURAL SPRING WENT BOOOOM!!
TRULY!! A MIRACULOUS MYSTERY BORN OF NATURE'S WHIMS!!
OKAY, JUST... CALM DOWN.

IF AN INJURED MAGICAL GIRL BATHES IN THAT WATER...
IT'S SAID THAT HER ETHEREAL BODY WILL HEAL.
HOW DO YOU KNOW ABOUT SUCH A WONDERFUL PLACE?

IT WAS IN (ELDER) CHIYODA-SAN'S NOTES.
?
AH...I GAVE HER THE NOTEBOOKS AND MEMOS MY SISTER LEFT BEHIND.
I COULDN'T MAKE HEADS OR TAILS OF THEM.

I'M DECIPHERING THEM SLOWLY BUT SURELY, HO HO!
A HEALING SPRING SOUNDS LIKE SOMETHING FROM A GAME! I WANT TO SEE IT!!
YES, INDEED.

CHIYODA-SAN'S GOT SOME PRETTY DARK STAINS, SO SHE NEEDS A VIGOROUS WASHING.
IT'LL HELP.
くるり
SCRUBBA
COULD YOU NOT MAKE ME SOUND LIKE DIRTY LAUNDRY?

FRIENDS WITH PIGEONS AND SUCH

HERE, I PUT THE LOCATION DATA IN THE APP.
SCOOP UP SOME WATER FOR ME WHILE YOU'RE AT IT.
IT'S A KEY INGREDIENT IN ALCHEMY.

I'M TOO INDOORS-Y TO BRAVE THE MOUNTAINS IN THE SUMMER.
IT'S BETTER THAN SITTING IN THE CEILING IN THE SUMMER.
THANKS. I'LL CHECK IT OUT.

SORRY... BUT MIGHT I SIT OUT THIS TRIP?
HUH? WHY?!
I'VE GOT AN INTERVIEW FOR MY SCHOOL TRANSFER TODAY.

Mikan
HS Student:
Park Vagrant
IF I MISS IT, I CAN'T OFFICIALLY REGISTER...
AND I'LL LOSE MY STATUS AS A STUDENT.
I-I SEE. GOOD LUCK, THEN.

A SIGN IN THE WILDERNESS

WAIT... I'VE BEEN HERE BEFORE!
YOU HAVE?
Oku-Oku Tama
Deep Inner Tama
Damu
YEAH...I MISSED MY TRAIN STOP ONCE.*

LOOKS LIKE THAT AREA IS MY SISTER'S PRIVATE PROPERTY.
IT'S A LITTLE FAR, BUT WE JUST HAVE TO FOLLOW THE PATH.
OH, THERE'S A SIGN.

WARNING
Beyond this point is private property.
In order to protect its valuable resources,
I have set many traps in the area
to stop thieves, and also for fun.
But if you really must enter...
T-TRAPS? AND WAIT... "FOR FUN"??

But if you really must enter...go ahead and find the treasure!! I'm sure only my family and friends would come here, anyway!
Landlord Chiyoda
WHAT ON EARTH IS SHE SAYING?
I WONDER WHAT THAT'S SUPPOSED TO MEAN...

* See Volume 1.

UNSAFE ARRANGEMENTS

TRAPS TO STOP THIEVES, HUH?
MAGIC TRAPS AND FAMILIARS, I'LL BET.
F-FAMILIARS?!

KNOWING MY SISTER, WE'LL PROBABLY GET COMICALLY BEATEN UP, BUT NOT KILLED.
I'M WEAK RIGHT NOW, SO YOU FIGHT THEM, SHAMIKO.
I'M GONNA GET COMICALLY BEATEN UP?

OKAY, LET'S G--
OOOO?!!
MOMOOOO?!!
KA CRNCH

A SUPER-BASIC PITFALL TRAP!!
IT'S NOT EVEN MAGICAL!!

I SEE RIGHT THROUGH YOU!

LET'S KEEP MOVING. THIS IS A CHALLENGE FROM MY SISTER.
I'VE GOT TO GET THAT TREASURE!
AREN'T YOU GETTING A LITTLE TOO WORKED UP?
IT *IS* KIND OF ANNOYING.

YOU GO FIRST, SHAMIKO.
HEY, THAT'S NOT FAIR!
IT'S JUST TO KEEP US EVEN, PITFALL-WISE.

THIS IS TRAINING, TOO. A CHANCE TO TRY NEW THI--
NNYAAAA!!
MOMO——!!!

THAT "NYA" PART WAS PRETTY CUTE.
SO, THEY CAN COME FROM BEHIND, TOO?!

MOMO-SAN IN A FRUIT NET

LET'S JUST GO HOME.
DON'T GIVE UP, DARN IT!!
I MIGHT FALL INTO DARK-NESS.
RUSTLE

INTRO... INTROO... INTRU... DERS...! INTRUD-ERS!
LEAVE NOW... LEAVE NOW...
NOW NOW NOW NOW NOW NOW!

AH, NOW THAT'S MORE LIKE IT.
URRK...
WHAT THE HECK IS THAT? A JELLO MONSTER?
IT'S AN AUTO-MATIC FAMILIAR.

TIME TO FIGHT, SHADOW MIS-TRESS-SAN!
FWIP FWIP
WAAA-AAH! WHERE'D THIS BATTLE SCENE COME FROM?!

BECOME A DEMON WITH BATTLE-SHARP SENSES

IT'S ON A PRETTY WEAK SET-TING.
STAY CALM! THE ENE-MY'S NOT AS SCARY AS YOU THINK!
IT'S IM-PORTANT TO TAKE A GOOD LOOK AT YOUR OP-PONENT.

FAMILIARS HAVE A SORT OF CORE TOO, SO AIM FOR THAT.
TROT TROT TROT TROT
I DON'T KNOW WHERE THAT IIIIS!!
PLEASE GIVE ME A HIIINT!!

IT'S CLEARLY THAT PINK STONE IT'S WEAR-ING.
TRY A LIIITTLE HARDER TO FIND ITS WEAK POINT.
YOU'RE SO MEEE-EAN!!

AHA! LOOK! IT CAN'T CLIMB TREES!
LET'S JUST SIT HERE AND WAIT FOR IT TO GIVE UP!
WE WON'T BE ABLE TO AVOID THE TRAPS ONCE IT GETS DARK, SO THAT'S A NO.
FLAIL
FLAIL

AN UNCONVENTIONAL VICTORY

UH... UM... WEAK POINT?! I DON'T KNOW!
AH! I CAN JUST HIT IT IN A BUNCH OF PLACES!!
LET'S SEE...

STAFF OF SOMETHING-OR-OTHER...
MIKAN-SAN'S WEAPON, COPY MODE!!!

ぽむむむ
POOMMPH
HUH?!

I...I WOOOON!!
I NEVER FOUND THE WEAK POINT, BUT I STILL WON!
UM...I GUESS THAT WORKS? KIND OF?
シュウウ
WHOO
OOSH...

A DEMON'S SPOILS OF VICTORY

IT'S A LITTLE SHODDY, BUT YOU DID COPY MOST OF THE BOW'S ABILITIES.
HEH HEHHH—*
IT'S VERY CONVENIENT!!
THE PARTS LOOK ODD.
SURE, LET'S CALL IT THAT.

IT'S MY FIRST DEMON VICTORY! I DID IT!!
BY THE WAY, THE WEAK POINT WAS THAT PINK STONE.
OHHH, I SEE.

SO, CAN I TAKE THIS STONE HOME WITH ME?
SURE, WHY NOT? IT'S PROBABLY MY SISTER'S.
IT'LL BE MY TREASURE! I'LL POLISH IT EVERY DAY!!

HEY, LET'S BRING HOME SOME DIRT FROM THE SITE OF MY VICTORY, TOO.
MOMO, CAN YOU TAKE A PICTURE?
WHAT ARE YOU, A LITTLE LEAGUE PLAYER?

A DEMON'S NEWLY DISCOVERED DESIRE

WE MAAADE IT!
SO, THIS IS CHIYODA SAKURA'S SECRET SPRING.

......
BLOOSH
IT'S KIND OF...A WATER-FALL.
YEP, THAT'S A WATER-FALL.
BURBLE
BURBLE

ARE YOU SKINNY DIPPING? BROUGHT A SWIM-SUIT?
OR DO YOU HAVE A FLOWING WHITE GOWN, OR A LOIN-CLOTH?
ARE YOU STUPID?! I'M KEEP-ING MY CLOTHES ON!

WOOOW!
IT'S SO MUCH FUN WATCHING MOMO STAND UNDER A WATER-FALL!!
COULD YOU STOP WAG-GLING YOUR TAIL SO MUCH?

MOMO'S MAGIC POINTS WERE RESTORED!!

MOMOOO! HOW'S IT GOING? ANY BAD THOUGHTS SO FAR?

NOPE, NONE.

AH HA HA HA!

......

BLOOSH BLOOSH BLOOSH

YOU GET REALLY ANNOY-ING WHEN YOU'RE CONFI-DENT!!
SPLASH
GYAH!!

HEY LOOK, MOMO-- YOU'RE GLOWING.
I DO FEEL ENERGIZED. I GUESS IT REALLY DOES WORK.

I WONDER IF I COULD INSTALL ONE OF THESE AT MY PLACE...
AH, BUT I THINK THE LOCATION IS PART OF THE POWER.
EVEN UNDER THE WATERFALL, SHE'S HAVING EVIL THOUGHTS.

CASUAL THEFT

THANKS FOR GETTING ME SO MUCH WATER!
IT WASN'T EASY.
WHY HAVE YOU MADE A LAB IN MY KITCHEN?
BECAUSE THE KITCHEN WAS THERE!

MMM... WHAT'S THAT?
MY SPOILS FROM THE MOUNTAIN!
BUT THAT'S... NAAH! IT CAN'T BE!!

A-AMAZING! IT'S TOP-QUALITY PINK JADE!!
THAT'S A VALUABLE SUPER-ULTRA-POWER STONE!!
LOOM
WHAAA?! IS IT REALLY ?!
IT'S EVEN BETTER THAN SPIRIT WATER!
EEK!

IT'S MY TREASURE!
THANK YOOOU!!
HEEEY!
YOINK!!

MEMORY, CRUSHED

THIS IS THE BEST GIFT EVER!!
YOU GUYS ARE JUST SO GREAT!
AAAAH, BUT THAT'S MY VERY SPECIAL TREASURE!

NOW... WITH THIS... I CAN MAKE MY BEST MEDICINE YET!
CRUNCH CRUNCH CRUN
WAIT AND SEE, SHAMIKO-CHAAAN!!
AAAAAAH!!

MY TREASURE...

WELL, THE MEMORY WILL BE IN YOUR HEART FOREVER.
I'LL KICK HER OUT BY THE END OF THE DAY.
THAT'S NOT GONNA CUT IT!
DON'T GIVE UP, SHAMIKO! YOU CAN AT LEAST PUT THE DIRT IN A NICE BOTTLE!!

The Demon Girl Next Door

The Demon
Girl
Next Door

I'VE GROWN RATHER USED TO LIVING ALONE...
BUT THIS MESS IS UNBE-COMING OF A LADY.

HRMM...
Kingdom: *Animalia* Phylum: *Arthro-poda* Class: *Insecta*
Order: *Blattodea* Common Name:

I DON'T KNOW HOW THE RECY-CLING IS HAN-DLED HERE.
I'LL HAVE TO LOOK UP THE SCHED-ULE.
HMM?

!!
...!!

AS LONG AS IT CAN'T HURT ME

SHAMIKOOOOO!!
GOOD MORNING, MIKAN-SAN.
GOOD DAY TO YOU! I SAW ONE! I SAW ONE!!

YOU KNOW THE ONE! THAT SPEEDY, BLACK, SMOOTH THING!
AHHH, A COCK-ROACH, HUH?
HOW CAN YOU SAY THAT SO CALMLY?!

AT LEAST CALL IT BY A CUTE-SIER NAME, LIKE "C-CHAN"!
WAIT, DO INSECTS NOT BOTHER YOU?
THIS BUILDING HAS LOTS OF CRACKS...
SO YOU GET USED TO RO-DENTS AND BUGS.

COCK-ROACHES HAVE NO ATTACK POWER, SO THEY'RE NOT SCARY!!
YOUR STANDARDS ARE SO BAFFLING AT TIMES!
MOMO IS MUCH SCARIER!!

LONG-HORNED BEETLES ARE DANGEROUS

HERE YOU GO.
?
WHAT'S THIS?
Skott

?
TISSUES, SO YOU CAN GRAB THE COCK-ROACH AND TAKE IT OUT-SIDE.
GRAB IT?!
WHY, I NEVER!!
Skott

BUT COCK-ROACHES DON'T BITE OR STING.
NOT LIKE HORSE-FLIES, BEES, LONG-HORNED BEE-TLES...
THAT ISN'T THE PROB-LEM HERE!
THOUGH THEY DIDN'T REALIZE IT AT THE TIME...

MIKAN'S CURSE...
WAS HITTING MOMO-SAN!!
MMPH!!

A SENSE OF SYMPATHY

I CAN'T STAND THOSE HORRID THINGS!
I DON'T SUPPOSE YOU'D HELP ME TIDY UP, SO I'M LESS FRIGHTENED?

NO PROBLEM! IF A COCKROACH SHOWS UP, I'LL GRAB IT.
YOU DON'T NEED TO GRAB IT! WHY WOULD YOU?!
Skott
Skott
SWFF

C-CHANS ARE QUITE FILTHY, YOU KNOW! IT'S BEST NOT TO TOUCH THEM.
SHOOM
NEXT TIME, I'LL BE READY, SEE?
SO, YOU'RE GOING TO DO AWAY WITH IT?

THEY GET CRUSHED JUST FOR SHOWING UP OR BEING BORN...
JUST LIKE DEMONS, POOR THINGS.
AA-ARGH, ALL RIGHT, ALREADY!
I'LL FIND A WAY TO RELEASE IT WITHOUT GRABBING IT!

GRABBY DEMON

LOOKS LIKE C-CHAN IS STILL HIDING.
IT RAN INTO A CORNER BEHIND THE GARBAGE.
OH DEAR, AND I HAVEN'T FIXED THIS DOOR YET...

I'M SORRY ABOUT THAT.
WE BROKE YOUR DOOR, MADE CRAZY DEMANDS--
IT'S PERFECTLY FINE.

IT WAS AN EMERGENCY, RIGHT?
INSTEAD OF "SORRY," JUST SAY, "THANK YOU."
AS LONG AS YOU'VE GOT MY BACK IF I NEED HELP.

OKAY! THEN ONCE C-CHAN POPS OUT, I'LL--
PLEASE DON'T GRAB IT!
Skott
Skott
SWFF

A MORTAL ENEMY WHO WANTS STAYING POWER

I'LL ADMIT I WAS A LITTLE WOR-RIED.
MOMO ALWAYS SEEMS TO ASK YOU TO DO CRAZY THINGS.

GOOD-NESS, IS *THAT* ALL?
IT'S FINE!
MOMO AND I KNOW EACH OTHER QUITE WELL.

WE'VE BEEN DOING CRAZY THINGS FOR EACH OTHER FOR TEN YEARS...
AL-THOUGH I'VE NEVER SEEN HER LOOK THIS DOUR BEFORE.
TEN YEARS!

WELL, WELL, WELL. ARE YOU JEAL-OUS?
O-OF COURSE NOT! SHE'S MY MORTAL ENEMY, DARN IT *AAALL!!*

A DEMON'S GARBAGE DUNK

COME TO THINK OF IT, THOUGH...
IT'S ONLY BEEN ABOUT THREE MONTHS SINCE I MET MOMO.

THERE MUST BE SO MANY STORIES THAT I DON'T KNOW.
I'LL NEVER BE ABLE TO SHARE THOSE WITH HER.
THAT DOES KIND OF... STING.

WAIT...
COULDN'T I PEEK AT THEM A LITTLE?
I AM A DREAM DEMON!

NO, NO, NO, NO, NO!
BAD, BAD, BAD, BAD, BA-AAD!!
THWACK THWACK THWACK
YOU'RE REALLY SHOWING THAT TRASH WHAT'S WHAT, AREN'T YOU?!
I'M TAKING OUT MY INNER TRASH, TOO!!

SOUNDS HANDY FOR ORANGE PEELS, TOO

AH, COULD I HAVE THESE OLD FLYERS?
? CERTAINLY, BUT WHATEVER FOR?
I MAKE LITTLE TRASH BINS WITH THEM.

SORRY, WHAT?
YOU KNOW, LIKE THIS!
YES, BUT WHY?!

THEY'RE GREAT FOR COLLECTING SCRAPS WHILE YOU'RE COOKING!
WHY, THAT'S INGENIOUS!!
I KNOW, RIGHT?!

ALSO, YOU CAN MAKE THROWING STARS...
AND ORIGAMI POP-GUNS AND STUFF!!
PEW
I'M SORRY, I DON'T UNDERSTAND WHAT THOSE ARE FOR!
PEW

ORIGAMI POP-GUNS ARE GREAT FOR RETORTS

AH!!
MIKAN-SAN, LOOK OUT! IT'S C-CHAN!!
WHAAAAT?!
SKITTER SKITTER

SMACK!!
QUICKLY, LET ME GRAB IT!
HOIST
I KEEP TELLING YOU, DON'T GRAB IT!!

CAN'T YOU SNEAK INTO C-CHAN'S DREAMS AND ORDER IT TO GO AWAY?!
I'D HAVE TO GO INTO A DEEP SLEEP FIRST.
THEN LIE DOWN! RIGHT HERE AND NOW!
EXCUSE ME...

COULD SOMEONE EXPLAIN WHY I'M GETTING HIT WITH MIKAN'S CURSE?
MOMO?!

MOMO-SAN LEARNS AN EASY WAY OUT

MY WATER PIPES BURST, THERE ARE HOLES IN THE GUTTER...
AND SHAMIKO FORGOT TO COOK MY RICE, SO I KNOW SOMETHING IS OFF.
YOU MAKE SHAMIKO COOK FOR YOU?

IF YOU ASK TOO MANY QUESTIONS, I'LL FALL INTO DARKNESS.
CONVERSATION OVER.
AH, THAT'S NOT FAIR! SNEAKY!!

BUGS, HUH? I CAN'T STAND THEM EITHER, LATELY.
NO FAIR! NO FAIR!
SMACK
ARE YOU AFRAID OF BUGS TOO, MOMO?
I HATE THE ONES WITH LEGS.
SMACK SMACK

FOR SOME REASON, I'VE STARTED GETTING CREEPED OUT WHEN I SEE THEM.
LIKE I WANT TO USE A FRESH PEACH HEART SHOWER.
SKITTER...
SKITTER...
SKITTER...
SKITTER...
SKITTER...
SHE'S STILL SCARRED FROM THAT CREEPY HOST BODY.

MAKING BOXES IS FUN

YOU CAN'T AVOID BUGS IN A RUN-DOWN BUILDING...
SO THIS ISN'T GONNA END WELL.
LET'S MAKE AN ANTI-BUG BARRIER.
"RUN-DOWN"?

LIKE THE ANTI-MAGICAL GIRL BARRIER AT YOUR HOUSE...
JUST A BIT SIMPLER.
RUN-DOWN?

IT TAKES SKILL TO MAKE A COMPLEX, STURDY BARRIER...
BUT MY SISTER TAUGHT ME HOW TO MAKE SIMPLE ONES.
DO YOU HAVE ANY EXTRA PAPER, MIKAN?

I DID...
BUT IT'S ALL TINY BOXES NOW.
WAIT, WHAT? WHY?

MANGA ASSISTANT LINGO GALORE

IT LOOKS LIKE A BLUE-PRINT.
YEAH ...
MAKING MAGIC CIRCLES IS A LOT LIKE ME-CHANICAL DRAFT-ING.

YOU FOLLOW THE RULES AND MAKE A DIA-GRAM.
SHA-MIKO, YOU DO THE CLEAN-UP.
WHAT KIND OF "CLEAN-UP"?!
ERASE THE EXTRA LINES.
Simple Black T-Shirt

I USED TO DO CLEAN-UP AND SPOT BLACKS* FOR MY SISTER'S BARRIERS.
WHAT DOES "SPOT BLACKS" MEAN?!

THREE HOURS LATER.
HERE! I MADE US COFFEE!
WHEN YOU LOOK AT IT FROM BEHIND, YOU CAN SEE THE FLAWS.
SAY, IS IT JUST ME, OR HAVE WE FOR-GOTTEN ABOUT C-CHAN?

* This is the process of adding solid black areas to a drawing, usually with ink.

A DEMON'S ULTIMATE FINISHING TOUCH

IS IT ALL DONE?
THERE'S STILL ONE STEP LEFT.

SHAMIKO, FILL THE IMAGE WITH MAGIC.
WHO, ME?!
JUST TOUCH IT WITH YOUR WEAPON AND FOCUS.

HI-YA——!!
FLASH!!

IT'S GLOWING!!
IT'S ACTI-VATED.
THAT MEANS WE'RE DONE.
POP
POP
POP
POP

A FLEETING FINISHING TOUCH

IF YOU PUT THIS ON THE DOOR, BUGS WON'T COME IN FOR A WHILE.
WHICH MEANS I'M SAFE!
THANKS SO MUCH, YOU TWO!
Hinatsuki

COME TO THINK OF IT...
YOU SAID, "FOR A WHILE."
DOES THAT MEAN THE BARRIER WILL EXPIRE?

HOW LONG IT LASTS DEPENDS ON THE QUALITY OF THE MAGIC IT'S CHARGED WITH.
THE QUALITY OF...
THE MAGIC?

NOT EVEN HALF A DAY.
THE QUALITY OF THE MAGIC...
NYO-OOO! IT'S BAAA-ACK!!

BECOME A DEMON WHO DOESN'T FALL ASLEEP MID-TRAINING

HI-YAAA-AH!
OKAY, NEXT ONE.
YAAAAAH!!
OKAY, NEXT ONE.

HERE ARE TEN NEW BARRI-ERS.
WHAT IS THIS, BOTTOM-LESS COFFEE?!
AND WHY AM I SO EX-HAUST-ED?!

WAIT A SECOND... COULDN'T MIKAN-SAN DO THIS IN-STEAD?!
I WOULD LOVE TO HELP...
BUT THE MORE MAGIC YOU USE THE EASIER IT GETS. THIS IS GOOD TRAINING FOR YOU.

IF YOU IMPROVE THE QUALITY OF YOUR MAGIC, YOU'LL ONLY HAVE TO DO ONE SHEET A MONTH!
I... I'M SO SLEEE-EEPY...
I MADE ORANGE TEA~!
DON'T GIVE UP, SHAMIKO! SURVIVE THIS TRAINING AND BECOME A HIGH-QUALITY DEMON!!

SECONDS!!
DEMON GIRL NEXT DOOR
(CHAPTER 45)
~ OGURA-SAN IS AN INDOOR PERSON

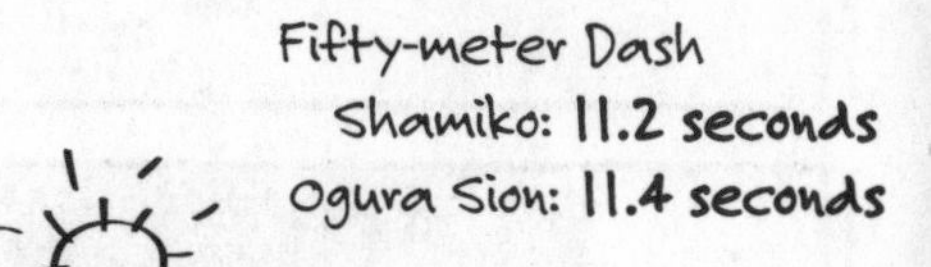
Fifty-meter Dash
Shamiko: 11.2 seconds
Ogura Sion: 11.4 seconds

THE SUN IS FAR TOO BRIGHT!

THERE'S A PLACE WHERE YOU CAN GET ALL BETTER ...
ZA
NWOOP...
T...
OGURA-SAN?!

HERE'S THE THING, THOUGH.
?

I'M A LITTLE HIGHER UP THAN I EXPECTED...
SO, COULD YOU MAYBE HELP ME DOWN?
WHAT, YOU DIDN'T RE-HEARSE THIS?
NO, TOO EXCITED.

I'LL BRING A LADDER NEXT TIME.
YOU'RE PLAN-NING TO DO THIS AGAIN?

SECONDS!!
DEMON GIRL NEXT DOOR
(CHAPTER 46)
~ THE SIMPLE BLACK T-SHIRT ~

I DON'T HAVE ANY GOOD GOING-OUT CLOTHES.
THIS OUTFIT FEELS KINDA WEIRD.
HMM... YOU'D LOOK BEST IN SOMETHING LIKE A SIMPLE BLACK T-SHIRT, DON'T YOU THINK?

I GOT ADVICE FROM MIKAN, BUT HONESTLY...
HOW AM I SUPPOSED TO FIND--

Simple Black T-Shirt
......!!

I'LL TAKE THIS IN A LARGE, PLEASE!
NAILED IT!!
DON'T GIVE UP, MAGICAL GIRL! GET THROUGH THE SUMMER IN SIMPLE OUTFITS!!

MOM'S PAPERCRAFT IS AMAZING!

YUKO ...
THE TIME HAS COME FOR YOU TO USE THE TRUE POWER OF YOUR FATHER'S STAFF!
AYE AYE, MA'AM!

IT'S GREAT BEING ABLE TO DRY THREE FUTONS AT ONCE!
I'M SO GLAD I'M A DEMON!

STAFF OF SOMETHING-OR-OTHER ...
CLOTHES-DRYING POLE MODE!
GET YER BAMBOO LAUNDRY POLE HEEERE!

DO YOU HAVE ANY BLANKETS I CAN DRY FOR YOU, MOMO?
CAN'T YOU THINK OF A MORE APPROPRIATE USE FOR THAT STAFF?

IF IT HAS A HANDLE, IT'S A STAFF

YOU SMELL SO NICE, MOMO.
LIKE A PEACH.
THAT'S BECAUSE THE WAVES OF MY ETHEREAL BODY MAKE YOU THINK--
WAIT! DON'T CHANGE THE SUBJECT!

ポフ
POOF
THAT STAFF IS SUPPOSED TO PROTECT YOU, SHAMIKO.
YOU SHOULD FIND MORE PRACTICAL USES FOR IT.
PRACTICAL...

WHAT'S THAT?
AN IDOL FAN!
TURN IT BACK RIGHT NOW.
MOMO-CHAN: FALL INTO DARKNESS

WAIT... A FAN ISN'T EVEN A STAFF!!
ISN'T IT, IN A WAY, THOUGH?!
WHAT IS GOING ON IN THAT BRAIN OF YOURS?!

IGNORANTLY BLISSFUL DEMON

FIRST OF ALL, THE "TRANSFORMS INTO ANYTHING STAFF-LIKE" RULE IS TOO VAGUE.
WHY CAN IT BECOME SO MANY THINGS?

A STAFF IS...
"A LONG, THIN POLE OF WOOD OR METAL, WIELDED BY HAND."
SO, THIS TECHNICALLY ISN'T A STAFF?!
MOMO-CHAN: FALL INTO DARKNESS
Japanese Dictionary

ポシュ
PWOOSH
H-HUH?! IT CHANGED BACK!
AH! SO, IT WON'T WORK IF SHAMIKO HAS DOUBTS.

DARN.
I SHOULD'VE JUST LET YOU KEEP BEING AN OBLIVIOUS IDIOT.
HEY, RUDE!

THE CHEAT WEAPONS OF THE WORLD

IN DREAMS, ONE CAN MAKE "OVER-POWERED WEAPONS" THAT CAN DEFEAT ANYTHING.
!
YOU MEAN, YOU COULD MAKE THINGS THAT AREN'T REAL? LIKE FICTIONAL WEAPONS?

I-I WANT TO SEE!
ITENKEN! GUNGNIR! AME-NO-NUHOKO!
HUH? WHAT ARE YOU TALKING ABOUT?

ITENKEN IS A SWORD FROM CHINESE MYTHOLOGY THAT CAN SLICE THROUGH SOLID ROCK!
GUNGNIR IS A SPEAR FROM NORSE MYTHOLOGY THAT NEVER MISSES AND ALWAYS COMES BACK!
WH-WH-AAA?

AME-NO-NUHOKO IS A MYTHICAL SPEAR THAT CAN STIR UP CHAOS AND GIVE IT FORM!!
WHAT DOES "STIR UP CHAOS" MEAN?!
WHEN AM I GONNA BUMP INTO CHAOS?!
Ame-no-Nuhoko
Attack Power

PEACH ALCHEMY

WEAPONS THAT AREN'T REAL... SHAMIKO, TRY MAKING A THIRTY-KILOMETER-LONG STAFF.
THIRTY KILOMETERS?!
I WANT TO SEE IF IT'LL BREAK THROUGH THE STRATOSPHERE.
IF IT STARTS TO TOPPLE OVER, I'LL FIGURE SOMETHING OUT.

HI... HI-YAAAAAH!
NOTH ING...
I... I CAN'T.

NOW TRY MAKING A SET OF PURE GOLD CHOPSTICKS.
B-BUT WHY?
I WANT TO SEE WHAT WOULD HAPPEN IF WE SOLD ONE CHOPSTICK, THEN TURNED THEM BACK.
MOMO!

I... I CAN'T. NORMAL WOODEN CHOPSTICKS I CAN DO, THOUGH.
SO, I GUESS CHEAT MOVES ONLY WORK IN DREAMS.
WHY WOULD YOU EVEN *THINK* OF THAT?

PLEASE HOLD ME PROPERLY

I IMAGINE THAT SHAMIKO HERSELF IS SUBCONSCIOUSLY LIMITING THE STAFF.
MOMO!
NOR DOTH SHE HAVE THE POWER TO MAKE SUCH WILD THINGS REAL.

THY HOME FIELD IS IN DREAMS!
WHY NOT PRACTICE WITHIN MY SEAL SPACE?

BY TRAINING IN DREAMS AND BRINGING ME INTO THE REAL WORLD...
THOU MAYEST CREATE MORE CHALLENGING THINGS.
O-OH, I SEE!

METHINKS THE GOLDEN CHOPSTICKS ARE A GRAND IDEA, TOO.
HEH HEH!
HEH HEH!
I'M NOT GOING TO DO THAT!

STANDS FOR "HOST BODY COUPONS"

DOST THOU WISH TO WATCH AS WELL, RYO?
IS THAT POSSIBLE?
THOU ART RELATED TO ME BY BLOOD, SO I CAN SUMMON THEE.

YES, PLEASE! I WANT TO SEE MY SISTER WIELDING LEGENDARY WEAPONS AGAINST VAST ARMIES!!
DON'T SET THE BAR TOO HIGH, PLEASE!

WHAT ABOUT ME, LILITH-SAN?
SINCE THOU ART NOT MY KIN, I CANNOT SUMMON THEE.
......

H.B.C.
SWF
I WANT THEM MORE THAN I CAN SAY...
BUT I PHYSICALLY CANNOT!
ASK AGAIN AFTER THOU HAST FALLEN INTO DARKNESS!

DEMON SWITCH ON

I AM PLEASED TO SEE THEE, DEAR DESCENDANTS!
It hath been too long! Worship me!

YOU'RE BLONDE!!
AH YES, THIS IS THY FIRST TIME SEEING MY TRUE FORM.
IMPRESSIVE, AM I NOT? PRAISE ME TO THY HEART'S CONTENT!

YOU'RE LIKE A 2P COLOR VERSION OF MY SISTER!
OF WHAT DO YOU SPEAK?

A 2P COLOR VERSION IS A TERM IN FIGHTING GAMES FOR WHEN TWO PLAYERS PICK THE SAME CHARACTER SO ONE OF THEM HAS AN ALTERNATE COLOR SCHEME SO THE PLAYERS CAN TELL WHO'S WHO
SHAMIKO, THOU ART SPEAKING QUITE QUICKLY!

SPARRING PARTNERS OR SANDBAGS?

BUT IN THIS CASE, I WAS BORN LATER, SO IT'S MORE LIKE YOU'RE THE 1P COLOR VERSION.
THAT WAS QUITE A SPEECH, SHAMIKO.
SORRY, I JUST REALLY LIKE VIDEO GAMES.

WELL, NO MATTER! PREPARE THY STAFF AT ONCE!
THIS IS THE DREAM REALM OF A GREAT DREAM DEMON.
I SHALL CREATE PERFECT TARGETS FOR THEE!

ONE HUNDRED LILITH SPARRING SANDBAGS...
COME ON DOWN!!!
TROMP
TROMP
TROMP
TROMP

I MADE THIS ARMY WITH MINE OWN HANDS IN MY RECENT PROLONGED DOWNTIME!
NOW, TURN THEM ALL TO DUST WITH THY STAFF!
WERE YOU *THAT* LONELY, ANCESTOR?!

DEMON WARRIORS

HI-YAA, HI-YAH!!
SMACK
THERE ARE STILL SO MANY!
SMACK

THOU HAST 29,950 LEFT TO GO!
THAT'S TOO MANY!
HOW LONELY *WERE* YOU, ANYWAY?!

I GET LONELY EASILY, IF THOU MUST KNOW!
IF THOU CAN'ST NOT BEAT THEM ALL, THOU MUST TAKE ME TO AN AMUSEMENT PARK.
I CAN TAKE YOU THERE ANYWAY!

BY THE WAY, I'VE ADDED A KILL COUNTER AT THE BOTTOM RIGHT.
?!
THE BOTTOM RIGHT OF *WHAT*?!
00051 K.O.

NOT ENOUGH IN THE BUDGET

THOU ART MOVING TOO SLOWLY! AT THIS RATE, THY BODY WILL WAKE UP!
RYO, ADVISE THY SISTER.
SHAMIKO HATH NO SENSE FOR WEAPONS.
00103 K.O.

UM, SIS, YOU'LL GET WORN OUT SWINGING THAT THING AROUND.
SINCE THIS IS A DREAM, I THINK YOU COULD USE A FAIRY-TALE WEAPON...

LIKE A SWORD THAT VAPORIZES WHOLE CONTINENTS WITH ONE STRIKE!
WHY DON'T YOU IMAGINE SOMETHING LIKE THAT?
VAPORIZES CONTINENTS!

IT'S NO USE! IT CAME OUT LIKE A DOODLE!
Continent Sword
SORRY, RYO. I CAN'T DO IT.
YOUR BIG SIS ISN'T IMAGINATIVE ENOUGH TO VAPORIZE CONTINENTS!
00107 K.O.

SNACK TIME IS IMPORTANT

LIKE A STAFF THAT MAKES MAGIC?
THEN WHY DON'T YOU TRY SOMETHING FROM ONE OF YOUR FAVORITE GAMES?
OOH...I THINK I CAN DO THAT!

ROD OF FIRE!
ROD OF THUNDER!
00650 K.O.

SNACK-BREAK STAFF!
IS THAT NECESSARY?
01090 K.O.

SHOOM
SHOO
FOR SOME REASON, THE SNACK-BREAK STAFF BEAT A BUNCH OF THEM.
I GUESS SWEETS ARE A POTENT WAY TO DISPEL LONELINESS.
10074 K.O.

QUEST COMPLETE

LAST ONE!!
ICE ROD!!
SHE TRULY DID DEFEAT THEM ALL!
I THINK... I'VE GOTTEN THE HANG OF IT!!
30000 K.O.

'TIS ALL THANKS TO THY ADVICE, RYO.
I ENJOYED MEETING THEE TODAY.
IN FACT... 'TWAS THE GREATEST BOON OF THIS DAY.

THOU ART SUCH A DARLING!
WORK HARD WITH THY SISTER TOWARDS A BRIGHTER FUTURE FOR OUR CLAN!
RIGHT!

CAN I TAKE YOUR PICTURE, ANCESTOR-SAMA?
I DOUBT A PHOTO IN THE DREAM WORLD WOULD SHOW UP IN REALITY...
NAY... WAIT A MOMENT. PERHAPS...

THE KIND YOU SEE ON ALTARS

MYAHH...
ART THOU BOTH AWAKE?
PLACE THY CAMERA BEFORE ME.

ABRACADABRA!
NNGH!
CLICK

WHAT EXACTLY DID YOU JUST DO?
Bwa ha ha... etc.!
I'VE BEEN PRACTICING, SINCE MY SEAL HATH WEAKENED...
SENDING AN IMAGE FROM THE SEAL SPACE TO THE WORLD BEYOND.
A SPIRIT PHOTO!

THOU NEEDEST ONLY ENLARGE MY IMAGE, FRAME IT, AND ADMIRE IT!
I FEEL LIKE THAT ISN'T QUITE RIGHT.

BECOME A DEMON WHO'S PHOTOGENIC

GOOD MORNING. HOW'D IT GO?
I GOT SOME GREAT PRACTICE!
AND... WE MADE SOME NICE MEMORIES, TOO.

YOU TOOK A PICTURE OF LILITH-SAN'S TRUE FORM?
THOU MAYEST USE IT AS A REFERENCE FOR MY HOST BODIES.
AH! THERE REALLY IS SOMETHING HERE!

NGRSJFSLKILDDME.jpg
......

EEK!!
SPIRIT PHOTOGRAPHY, HUH?
IT SEEMETH THAT I MAY NEED A BIT MORE PRACTICE.

DON'T GIVE UP, LILITH-SAN! PUT IN SOME WORK TO BECOME A PHOTOGENIC DEMON!

SECONDS!!
DEMON GIRL NEXT DOO
(CHAPTER 45)
~ MIKAN-CHAN CAN'T ESCAPE ~

WHAT ABOUT YOUR HOMEWORK, MIKAN-SAN?
SINCE I'M TRANSFERRING HERE IN SEPTEMBER...

THE HOMEWORK FROM MY OLD SCHOOL WON'T FOLLOW ME...
AND I CAN HAVE FUN ALL SUMMER LONG!!
IT'S A SPECIAL PERK OF BEING A TRANSFER STUDENT!
ドヤ
SMUUUG

WOW, I'M SO JEALOUS!!
OOOH HO HO HO!
WHY, I CAN'T STOP MYSELF FROM OH-HO-HO-ING!!
OOOH HO HO!
OOOH HO HO HO!

ENTRANCE INTERVIEW.
NOW, MIKAN.
I'VE PREPARED SOME PRACTICE WORK.
THIS WILL ALL BE COVERED ON THE BACK-TO-SCHOOL TESTS.
OH, DRAT.

I CAME FROM AROUND HERE.
Around here.*

* Based on this map, Mikan is from the Hiroshima area.

MOMO!! LET ME SQUEEZE THAT WEIRD THING ON YOUR HEAD.
WHY?
PUFF
PUFF

SECONDS!!
DEMON GIRL NEXT DOOR
(CHAPTER 47)
~ PEACH PUFF AIR FRESHENER ~

SQUEEZ-ING IT MAKES THE PEACH SCENT STRONG-ER...
WHICH MAKES MY RICE TASTE EVEN BETTER!
I'M TAKING THIS OFF.

I DON'T LIKE BEING USED TO FLAVOR RICE.
......

WOULD FLAVORING BREAD BE OKAY, THEN?

IT CHANGED COLOR
AFTER I FELL INTO DARKNESS
THE FIRST TIME, BUT IT'S
(PROBABLY) FINE.

A summer full of fun and mystery comes to an end...
and the new school term begins!!

I HOPE I CAN INTRO-DUCE MYSELF PROP-ERLY.
WILL PEOPLE BE PUT OFF IF I MENTION MY CURSE?

DON'T WORRY. THEY'LL ACCEPT YOU.
I'M EXCIT-ED THAT YOU'RE IN MY CLASS, MIKAN-SAN!
IT'LL BE SO MUCH FUN!

MAYBE YOU COULD HOLD A MIKAN-CHAN DOLL WHILE YOU TALK.
OOH, OR I COULD CHEER YOU ON WITH POM-POMS!
NICE TO MEETCHA!
WOO!♪ WOO!♪
I THINK THAT WOULD FREAK PEOPLE OUT EVEN MORE!

YOUR EN-THUSIASM WILL JUST LAND MY CURSE ON YOU!
BARK BARK
I FORGOT THAT IT ACTIVATES IF YOU GET OVER-EXCITED, TOO!

WELCOME TO CLASS 1-D!

I'M HINATSUKI MIKAN, A MAGICAL GIRL!
IT'S A PLEASURE TO MEET YOU.
Hinatsuki Mikan

HINATSUKI-SAN HAS AN UNUSUAL NATURE, DUE TO AN ACCIDENT WHEN SHE WAS YOUNG.
IF SHE GETS UPSET, HER MAGIC DEFENSE SYSTEM...
CAUSES THE PEOPLE AROUND HER TO EXPERIENCE MINOR DISASTERS.

THIS IS TRIGGERED BY HER HEART RATE, INJURIES, AND THINGS LIKE THAT.
I KNOW IT'S A LITTLE WEIRD, BUT...I'LL DO MY BEST TO FIT IN!

SO, NO SURPRISES, HUH?
WHEN DO I SET OFF THE WELCOME POPPER, THEN?
THAT'S A NO-GO, ANRI-CHAN! PLEASE PUT IT AWAY!

THE SECRET OF THE RIBBON, REVEALED!

DOES ANYONE HAVE QUESTIONS FOR HINATSUKI-SAN?

YOU CAN ASK ME ANYTHING ABOUT MY CURSE OR ABOUT MAGICAL GIRLS!

WHAT DO YOU PUT ON YOUR EGGS?
WHAT DO YOU WASH FIRST WHEN YOU BATHE?
CAN YOU EAT FRIED FOODS EARLY IN THE MORNING?
YOU'RE ALL IGNORING THE FANTASY ELEMENTS?!

UM...YOU CAN ASK A BIT MORE ABOUT MY NATURE, IF YOU'D LIKE.
IN FACT, IT'S BEST IF YOU KNEW WHAT TO EXPECT.

HOW DOES THAT FUNNY RIBBON ON TOP OF YOUR HEAD WORK?
IT'S PART OF MY ETHEREAL BODY, SO I CAN MOVE IT AROUND BASED ON MY MOOD~! ♡
WAIT! YOU'RE STILL NOT TAKING THIS SERIOUSLY!!

COMPLETE WITH CAMERA FEATURES

BREAK PERIOD.
SHAMIKO! DID I DO ALL RIGHT?!
IT WAS THE BEST INTRODUCTION EVAH!!
CITRUS

YOU MOVED HERE TO GUARD SHAMIKO, RIGHT? YOU SURE ACT FAST.
INDEED! I'D LOVE TO GET YOUR CONTACT INFO, SATA-SAN.
SURE!! AND JUST CALL ME ANRI!

THAT THING WHERE YOU WAVE YOUR PHONES TOGETHER LOOKS FUN.
I WANT A CELL PHONE, TOO!
I DO THINK IT WOULD BE BEST IF YOU HAD ONE.
BUT THEY'RE REALLY PRICEY, RIGHT?

IT WOULD BE FREE IF YOU LET ME ADD CALL FEATURES TO LILITH-SAN!
I CALL FOUL ON THEE, OGURA.
PICK ME!!

PRINCESS OF TENNIS

ARE YOU GONNA JOIN A CLUB?
TENNIS IS GREAT--YOU SHOULD PLAY WITH ME!
I DO APPRECIATE THE INVITATION...

BUT MAGICAL GIRLS HAVE GREAT PHYSICAL PROWESS.
IT WOULDN'T BE FAIR IF WE PLAYED AGAINST REGULAR HUMANS.
WHOA! I GUESS CHIYOMOMO IS PRETTY POWERFUL, TOO.

DOESN'T THAT MAKE YOU WANNA SEE A MAGICAL GIRL TENNIS BATTLE, THOUGH?
PEACH TIME-SPACE RUPTURE SERVE!!
YES!! I WANT TO SEE THAT RIGHT NOW!!

MOMO!! LET'S GO OUTSIDE AND--
NO WAY.
THE FIRST SERVE WILL BREAK THE BALL AND END IT.
YOU NEED TO DREAM BIGGER, DARN IT!!

TRY A LITTLE HARDER, DEMON

SPEAKING OF SPORTS... FIELD DAY'S COMING UP.
I'M ON THE FIELD DAY COMMITTEE, TOO.
BASICALLY, TWO SCHOOL TEAMS COMPETE FOR POINTS. WHAT SHOULD I DO ABOUT YOU GUYS?

HOW FAST IS YOUR FIFTY-METER DASH?
ABOUT SIX SECONDS.
THREE SECONDS.
ELEVEN SECONDS FOR THIS DEMON!
DUDE, FOR REAL?

I THINK IT WOULD BE EASIEST NOT TO INCLUDE MAGICAL GIRLS.
AW, MAN...
I'M KINDA BUMMED YOU CAN'T JOIN IN, EVEN THOUGH YOU DID JUST TRANSFER HERE.

HOW ABOUT I DEVELOP A DRUG THAT TEMPORARILY SUPPRESSES THE POWERS OF MAGICAL GIRLS?!
NOW, THAT'S INTRIGUING!
WHOOPS, WE SUMMONED OGURAAA!

THE SIZE OF A LONG-LIVED MARIMO*

SORRY, SORRY! I ACTUALLY JUST CAME TO DELIVER THIS.
IT'S CHIYODA-SAN'S DARKNESS-STABILIZING MEDICINE.
OH, I SEE. WAIT...
DARKNESS-STABILIZING?!

I USED THAT LOVELY PINK JADE YOU GAVE ME THE OTHER DAY.
THANKS AGAIN FOR HAPPILY HANDING IT OVER, SHAMIKO-CHAN.
DID I DO THAT "HAPPILY"...?

IF CHIYODA-SAN FALLS INTO DARKNESS, THIS'LL PREVENT THE LOSS OF HER MAGIC.
TAKE IT WHEN YOU'RE IN A BIND.
THANK YOU SO MUCH!
MY TREASURED STONE CAME BACK IN SUCH A WONDERFUL FORM!

HOW AM I SUPPOSED TO TAKE THIS? IT'S TOO BIG TO SWALLOW!
AND YOU KNOW JADE IS A ROCK, RIGHT? WHAT ELSE IS IN HERE?
JUST CHEW IT UP AND SWALLOW IT.
ANSWER THE QUESTION!

A marimo "moss" ball is a type of fresh-water algae that grows into green, velvety spheres. The longer the algae lives, the larger the balls grow.

EXTREMELY NICHE COMMITTEES

All committees will be meeting today.
Please gather in your assigned --
OKAY, I'VE GOTTA GO.

COMMITTEES?
EVERYONE HAS TO JOIN A COMMITTEE AT OUR SCHOOL.
AH! THEY HAD THAT AT MY OLD SCHOOL, TOO.

SENSEEE!! MIKAN-CHAN ISN'T ON A COMMITTEE YET.
HMM, WHERE SHALL WE PUT HINATSUKI-SAN?
DO YOU HAVE A PREFERENCE?

YOU SHOULD JOIN THE HUMAN-BODY-MODEL-POLISHING COMMITTEE!
THE KUDZU-CULTIVATION COMMITTEE NEEDS MORE PEOPLE.
HOW ABOUT THE ZOMBIE-SURVIVAL-MANUAL COMMITTEE?
AREN'T THERE ANY *NORMAL* COMMITTEES?!

PEACHES TAKE THREE YEARS, ORANGES TAKE FIVE

AT OUR SCHOOL, STUDENTS CAN CREATE A COMMITTEE IF THEY FIND A JOB THAT NEEDS DOING.
AND YES, SOME OF THEM *ARE* A BIT ODD.
ISN'T THAT A LITTLE TOO MUCH FREEDOM?!

I'M ON THE HEALTH COMMITTEE.
WHY DON'T YOU JOIN, TOO? AT LEAST YOU'LL HAVE A FRIEND.
HRMM... I'M AFRAID MY CURSE MIGHT ACT UP IF I SEE INJURED PEOPLE.

SENSEI... MAY I CREATE AN ORANGE CULTIVATION COMMITTEE?
THEY'RE C-LICIOUS!
ORANGES, *HMM?* THAT DOES SOUND TASTY.
HOW LONG DO THEY TAKE TO BEAR FRUIT?

FROM A SEEDLING, FOUR OR FIVE YEARS.
YOUR PROJECT HAS TO BE DONE BEFORE YOU GRADUATE, I'M AFRAID.
I SIMPLY CAN'T WIN.

BECOME A CITRUS FRUIT WHO FITS IN THE CLASS

OH DEAR... WHATEVER SHALL I DO?
"I'm part of the Field Day Committee, too."
AH...

ERM... IF I MAY...!
PERHAPS I COULD JOIN THE FIELD DAY COMMITTEE, SATA-SAN!

ARE YOU SURE? IT'S PRETTY BUSY RIGHT NOW.
IN FACT, THAT'S WHY I HELD OFF ON INVITING YOU. IT CAN BE STRESSFUL.
IT'S ALL RIGHT! I DO SO ENJOY PLANNING EVENTS.

AND YOU SAID...
"I'M KINDA BUMMED YOU CAN'T JOIN IN, EVEN THOUGH YOU DID JUST TRANSFER HERE."
THIS WAY, I CAN HELP OUT BEHIND THE SCENES AND GET TO KNOW EVERYONE.

MUSCLE ACQUIRED

I'M SURE THERE'S LOTS TO DO WITH FIELD DAY COMING UP...
SO I'D LIKE TO WORK HARD, ALONG WITH YOU!
SWEET!! YOU'RE MORE THAN WELCOME!!

COULD YOU TALK TO THE REST OF THE COMMITTEE FOR ME, SATA-SAN?
YOU GOT IT~!
MIKAN-SAN... I'M SO GLAD!!

CAN'T WAIT TO WORK WITH YA!
ME TOO!

AND NOW, THERE'S NO ESCAPE!
YOUR MAGICAL GIRL STRENGTH WILL COME IN HANDY FOR SETTING THINGS UP.
CLENCH CLENCH
OH DEAR...THIS MIGHT BE HARDER THAN I THOUGHT.

IT'S SURPRISINGLY EASY TO GET LOST HERE

IS YOUR MEETING OVER?
YOU WAITED FOR US?
SURE DID! OUR MEETING ENDED EARLY.

I FIGURED I COULD BARGE IN TO HELP IF YOU HAD ANY TROUBLE!
I'M ALL RIGHT.
ANRI WAS KIND ENOUGH TO KEEP AN EYE ON ME.

THAT'S WHY ANRI-CHAN'S THE BEST!
HEH HEH.
SHE HELPED ME OUT THE FIRST TIME WE MET, TOO.
I WAS PRETTY FRAIL BEFORE MY HORNS GREW IN.

SO, ON MY VERY FIRST DAY HERE...
I GOT MAROONED AT SCHOOL AND COLLAPSED.
WHAT DO YOU MEAN, "MAROONED"?

THE FIRST MEETING WITH ANRI-CHAN, REVEALED!

Hey, you okaaay? Feeling sick?
You a new first-year?
Yes.
I got lost... and then... my throat started closing up...

You got lost at school? That's pretty cool!!
Wanna go see the nurse?
I want...to attend the entrance ceremony. I'll be fine if I can sit down.
Then I'll get you to the auditorium!

Ta-daaa! Your carriage has arrived!!
Hop on, Missy!
Um... okay.

Just ask a teacher for help next time.
I'm sorry.
I THOUGHT SHE WAS REALLY... UNUSUAL.

PEACH CAT PARTY

YOU'VE GOT A LOT MORE ENERGY NOW THAN YOU DID BACK THEN, SHAMIKO...
AND YOU'RE BETTER AT SNAPPY COMEBACKS!
I WANT TO BE PRAISED FOR MY STRENGTH, NOT MY COMEBACKS!
A SUMMER FULL OF FUN AND MYSTERY HAS COME TO AN END.

THINGS HAVE GOTTEN MUCH LIVELIER THAN THEY WERE IN OUR FIRST TERM.
I HOPE I CAN KEEP MOVING FORWARD, LITTLE BY LITTLE.
I WONDER... WHICH COMMITTEE DID MOMO JOIN?
HUH? YOU GUYS GOING HOME?

AH, MOMO.
WHAT ARE YOU DOING?!

WORKING FOR MY COMMITTEE.
WHAT'S THAT?!
THE SURROUNDED-BY-CATS COMMITTEE.
WHAT KIND OF JOB IS THAT?!

HOW DID YOU SELL THAT TO THE TEACHER?

THERE WERE NO COMMITTEES I WANTED TO JOIN, SO I MADE MY OWN.

I DON'T SEE HOW THAT'S HELPFUL TO THE SCHOOL.

THAT'S NOT TRUE...IT'S A SUPER-IMPORTANT JOB!
LOOK ME IN THE EYES AND EXPLAIN.
....

I-I HAVE TO CHECK ON THE CATS WHO LIVE NEAR THE SCHOOL... TO MAKE SURE THEY'RE ALL...HEALTHY...
IN ORDER TO... PROTECT... UM...PEACE IN THE AREA?
NOW YOU'RE JUST LYING TO YOURSELF.

YOU'RE NOT ALLOWED TO SLACK OFF!
YOU CAN JOIN THE FIELD DAY COMMITTEE TOMORROW, CHIYOMOMOOO!
NO THANKS.
DON'T GIVE UP, MOMO-SAN! COME UP WITH A MORE CONVINCING EXPLANATION NEXT TIME!!

The Demon
Girl
Next Door

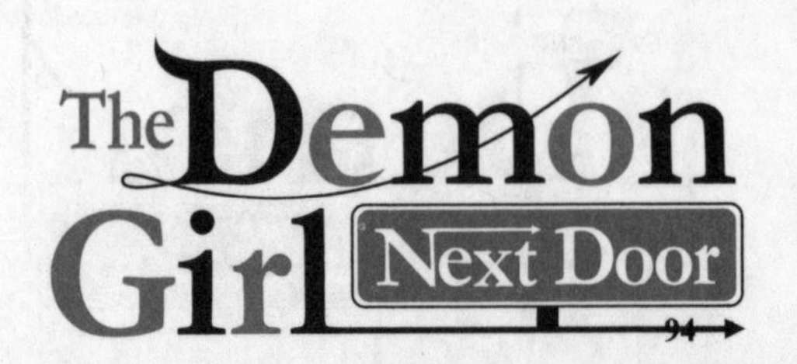
The Demon
Girl
Next Door
94

THIS IS JUST AWFUL!!
YEAH, THIS IS REAL BAD!!
WHAT'S THE MATTER, YOU TWO?

IT'S ALMOST TIME FOR FIELD DAY, BUT WE'RE NO-WHERE NEAR PRE-PARED.
WHY DOES OUR SCHOOL HAVE TO HAVE ITS FIELD DAY RIGHT AFTER SUMMER BREAK?!

PEOPLE CAN'T MEET UP DURING BREAK 'CAUSE OF SPORTS, CRAM SCHOOL ...
SUMMER BREAK IS WAY BUSIER THAN YOU'D THINK!!
I KNOW WHAT YOU MEAN!

I'M STILL EXHAUSTED FROM BEATING THIRTY THOUSAND ANCE-STATUES!
THIRTY THOUSAND WHAT, NOW?

A DEMON AVOIDS FLYING SOLO

WE'RE GONNA HAVE TO START STAYING AFTER SCHOOO-OOL!
I'M JUST GLAD MIKAN AND CHIYO-MOMO ARE HERE TO HELP OUT!

OH, DON'T MENTION IT! IT'S FUN TO MEET NEW PEOPLE.
I DON'T KNOW WHY I'M HERE. I WANT TO GO HOME AND SNUGGLE MY CAT.
MOMO'S HAVING FUN, TOO.

RIGHT, MOMO'S HELPING WITH FIELD DAY, TOO.
SO, THEY'LL BOTH GET HOME LATE.
ALL ALOOONE...
HM~~~...

ANRI-CHAN, I'LL HELP TOO, FOR NO REASON AT ALL!
THIS DEMON WILL ASSIST YOU WELL INTO THE NIGHT!!
WHERE'S THIS COMING FROM?! BUT THANKS, DUDE!!
GRAB!! ぱっ!!

A DEMON'S HEIGHT IS A SECRET

HELLO THERE~!
THANKS FOR THE HELP~!
※Field Day Management Committee (First-Years)

THE FIRST-YEARS' OUT-STANDING RESPONSI-BILITIES...
ARE MAKING PROPS AND SCEN-ERY...
TEST RUNS FOR EACH CONTEST, AND--
I SEE! THAT'S A LOT OF STUFF.

TELL ME WHEN THIS BREAD IS AT JUST THE RIGHT HEIGHT!
ぴょん HOP
HI-YA! HI-YAAA!!
ぴょん HOP
ぴょん HOP

SO, WE'LL SET THE HEIGHT FOR THE BREAD-EATING CONTEST AT 135 CENTI-METERS.
OOH, THAT ROLL LOOKS GOOD, TOO.
HANG ON!
YOU MIGHT WANT TO TRY USING SOME-ONE ELSE!!

I CAN USE RIGHT-HANDED ONES, TOO

MIKAN-SAN, DO THE TEST RUNS FOR ME, PLEEEASE!
IF THEY BASE THEM ON ME, THE GAMES WILL ALL BE TOO EASY!

WHAT ELSE NEEDS TO BE DONE?
LOOKS LIKE WE NEED SASHES FOR THE RELAY RACE.
GREAT, I'LL GO SEW SOME UP!

THEY'RE DONE ALREADY. TRY SOMETHING ELSE.
YRR RR RR RR
YOU'RE MOVING SO FAST!
I'VE GOTTEN PRACTICE FROM MAKING LILITH-SAN'S HOST BODIES.

ARE YOU STARTING TO ENJOY THIS A LITTLE?
NOT AT ALL. I JUST WANT TO FINISH UP QUICKLY.
Red Team
THIS EMBROIDERY SAYS OTHERWISE.

MOMO STAN

MIKAN-SAN LOOKS LIKE SHE'S HAVING FUN.
THANK GOODNESS!!

MIKAN-SAN'S REALLY COOL, ISN'T SHE?!
AND SHE'S GOT SUCH A GREAT FIIIGURE!
HER RUNNING FORM IS GREEEAT!

WOW, SHE'S GOT FANS~!
SHE'S SO CARING AND RADIANT... SHE'LL BE POPULAR IN NO TIME, I BET.
GAZE

BUT YOU'RE A CHIYO-MOMO FAN, EVEN IF SHE DOESN'T STAND OUT, RIGHT, SHAMIKO?
WHAT'S THAT SUPPOSED TO MEAN?! I'M NOT A "FAN"!!
AND... MOMO DOES STAND OUT--IN HER OWN WAY!!

ORANGES (AND MIKAN) CAN BE SOUR

MIKAN-SAN, ARE YOU DOING ALL RIGHT?
YES, BUT... ISN'T YOUR FACE A BIT RED?
NOT AT ALL, WHY?

I'M GLAD I FOUND A ROLE LIKE THIS. I SHOULD FIT IN SOON ENOUGH.
O-OH, UM, THAT'S GREAT!
MY DEAR... YOU KEEP GIVING ME WORRIED LOOKS.

IT'S EASY TO GET BY IN THIS TOWN.
IT'S LAID-BACK, AND EVERYONE'S OPEN-MINDED, IF A BIT ODD.
I CAN EVEN LIVE ON MY OWN. I'M GLAD I CAME.
IN OTHER WORDS...

I DIDN'T MOVE HERE JUST TO PROTECT YOU, YOU KNOW!
I'M HERE BECAUSE I WANT TO BE!
SO STOP WORRYING ABOUT ME ALREADY!
SMACK!!
Y-YES, MA'AM!

PEACH ENGINE IN OVERDRIVE

IF ANYONE'S FREE, PLEASE COME HEEERE!
I'D LIKE TO FINISH UP THIS MURAL!

OH, WOW!
FIRST-YEARS' BONDS
IT'S GOING ON THE OUTSIDE WALL, SO IT'S HUGE!

BUT WE GOT CARRIED AWAY, SO WE'RE RUNNING LATE.
WE WANTED TO KEEP THE QUALITY HIGH!
A LOT OF LOVE WENT INTO IT!!
THOSE JUST SOUND LIKE EXCUSES.

CHIYODA-SAN, YOU'RE SO GOOD AT PAINTING!!
I'VE GOTTEN PRACTICE FROM MAKING MAGIC CIRCLES.
SPLAT
SPLUT
SPLUT
MOMO... I'M GLAD YOU'RE HAVING FUN.

CHAIN REACTION

NOW IT JUST NEEDS TO DRY.
MIND IF I BORROW THIS PAINT?
GO AHEAAD!

MIKAN-SAN, WHAT'S IT FEEL LIKE ON THAT "MULE"?
IT DOESN'T FEEL TERRIBLY STABLE.
WE MIGHT WANT TO PAIR UP PEOPLE WITH SIMILAR HEIGHTS.

CAN YOU WALK?
I THINK SO--
BONK
AAAH?! SORRY!

EEEEK!!
AAAAAH!

MIKAN GOES OFF

MIKAN, YOU OKAY?!
......
WAIT!

DON'T GET TOO CLOSE TO HER!
WHEN MIKAN PASSES OUT, THAT'S WHEN...
HER CURSE REALLY GOES OFF!!

WHA... HUH?!
FWOOO
GET BEHIND ME!

THE MURAL IS SACRIFICED

I THINK... SHE'S CALMED DOWN NOW.
SHOOM
NNGH...
MIKAN-SAN, ARE YOU ALL RIGHT?!

UH-OOOH, THE MURAL.
First-Years' Bonds
I'M SO SORRY!

IT'S NOT YOUR FAULT, MIKAN-SAN!! I SHOULD'VE BEEN MORE CAREFUL WITH THE PAINT!
WAH!
WAH!
IT'S 'CAUSE I TRIED TO DO MULE FORMATION!
WAH!
HOW'S YOUR HEAD? ARE YOU OKAY?
WAH!

HERE, THIS FROZEN WATER BOTTLE SHOULD HELP.
IT WOULDN'T MELT, SO I DIDN'T KNOW WHAT TO DO WITH IT!
AH HA HA...HA...
WHIP!!

BECOME A DEMON WHO CAN FORM BONDS

GOOD WORK TODAY!

I THINK WE MIGHT ACTUALLY FINISH IN TIME!

LET'S CALL IT A DAY! IT'S SO DARK OUT!

MIKAN! SEE YOU TOMORROW!
I... COULDN'T DO ANYTHING.
LIKE WHEN THE MURAL GOT MESSED UP...

BACK-TO-NORMAL STAFF!!
THERE! IT'S BACK TO HOW IT WAAAS!!
OOOH!!

IT'S NOT WORKING...I GUESS THAT MAKES SENSE.
IT LOOKS LIKE I STILL DON'T HAVE ENOUGH POWER IN THE REAL WORLD.
CLASP...

THE CURSE THAT PROTECTS MIKAN ①

I'M... GOING ON AHEAD.
SHUFFLE...
AH...
MIKAN-SAN! WAIT!

IT WASN'T YOUR FAULT...
AND NO ONE'S UPSET, EITHER.
IN FACT, THEY SAID IT WAS KIND OF COOL AND FUN.
THE PEOPLE HERE REALLY ARE KIND.

I LOVE BOTH YOU AND MOMO...
AND AFTER TODAY, I'VE GROWN FOND OF OUR CLASSMATES, TOO.
THEN TOMORROW, WE CAN KEEP--
BUT...

THE CLOSER WE GET, THE MORE LIKELY THEY'LL GET HURT.
THE ONLY REASON NOBODY GOT INJURED TODAY IS BECAUSE MOMO HAPPENED TO BE THERE.

THE CURSE THAT PROTECTS MIKAN ②

MIKAN... LISTEN...
LEAVE ME ALONE FOR NOW, PLEASE.
IF MY FEELINGS SHIFT, WHO KNOWS WHAT SORT OF CURSE WILL BE UNLEASHED...
AND I DON'T WANT... TO CAUSE ANY MORE HARM.

THIS POWER...
AT FIRST, IT PROTECTED ME FROM BAD PEOPLE.
ONCE, I COULD EVEN TALK WITH THE BEING WITHIN ME...A LITTLE.

BUT... BECAUSE THE SUMMONING WAS DONE WRONG, THINGS GOT MORE CHAOTIC.
I TRIED TO FIND WAYS TO FIX IT...
BUT STILL... THINGS LIKE THIS ALWAYS HAPPEN WHEN I LET MY GUARD DOWN.

MIKAN... LET'S TALK ONCE YOU'VE CALMED DOWN.
YES... ONCE I'VE CALMED DOWN, INDEED.
WELL, GOOD NIGHT, THEN.

WHAT I CAN DO FOR YOU

"IT'S FINE! IT WAS AN EMERGENCY, RIGHT?
"AS LONG AS YOU'VE GOT MY BACK IF I NEED HELP."
......

EVEN IF I'M WEAK... AND SLOW... AND CLUELESS...
THERE MUST BE SOMETHING ONLY A DREAM DEMON LIKE ME CAN DO.

MOMO!
AH... SHAMIKO.

I WAS JUST ABOUT TO HEAD OVER TO YOUR PLACE.
SO, YOU WERE THINKING THE SAME THING!
THAT'S MY MORTAL ENEMY!

DEMON/MAGICAL GIRL ALLIED FORCES

MIKAN-SAN!
BAM
EEEEK!

WH-WHAT?! DON'T JUST BARGE INTO A LADY'S ROOM!
IT'S NOT JUST YOUR ROOM!
I'M ABOUT TO BARGE INTO YOUR MIND!

WHAT?
I'M GOING IN...
TO TALK TO THE DEMON THAT LIVES INSIDE YOU!

AND MY (TEMP) VASSAL IS COMING, TOO!!
UM... YEAH.
WHAAAAA?!
DON'T GIVE UP, SHAMIKO! FIGHT IN A WAY THAT ONLY DREAM DEMONS CAN!!

The story so far:
I want to fix Mikan-san's curse at its source!

I'M GOING TO BREAK INTO YOUR MIND, MIKAN-SAN!
WH-WHAT DOES THAT MEAN?

MAYBE IF I BRING IT A BOX OF CAKES... OR SOME DETER-GENT?
WHAT, LIKE YOU'RE A SALES REP?!
AND... WHY IS MOMO GOING WITH YOU?
KIRARA
INDOOR DRYING
CARAT

YOU SAID AT ONE POINT YOU COULD TALK WITH THE BEING INSIDE YOU.
SO, I'LL SEE IF I CAN PER-SUADE IT TO FIX THINGS.

IF SHA-MIKO'S AP-PROACH DOESN'T WORK ...
I'LL PER-SUADE IT WITH MY FISTS.
HEY, THAT'S NOT THE PLAN!
MOMO'S JUST MY BODY-GUARD!

A COZY ORGANIZATION

BODY-GUARD? WHY, IS THIS DANGEROUS?
TO BE FRANK, IT IS INDEED.
IT SHOULD BE EASY TO ENTER THY MIND WITH THY PERMISSION...

BUT THE ENTITY WITHIN THEE WILL SEE THESE TWO AS INTRUDERS.
THERE IS NO TELLING WHAT IT MIGHT DO.
THEN YOU MUSTN'T DO THIS AT ALL!
I'VE MANAGED TO GET BY ALL THIS TIME, MORE OR LESS--

NO, I HAVE TO!
CLENCH
IT'S PART OF A DARK EMPRESS'S JOB TO HANDLE PROBLEMS LIKE THIS ONE!

IN ORDER TO CREATE A DARK ORGANIZATION THAT PEOPLE WILL FLOCK TO, I HAVE TO OFFER UNIQUE EMPLOYEE BENEFITS!!
NOW HIRING
BFFs
Employee Benefits:
* Dream counseling
* Home-cooked meals
* A demon to solve all your problems
THAT SOUNDS MORE LIKE A START-UP!!

LOTS OF ACTIVE INGREDIENTS

SHAMIKO SAYS SHE WANTS TO HELP YOU...
AND I FEEL THE SAME WAY.
EVEN IF IT IS A LITTLE DANGEROUS, JUST TRUST US. WE'LL BE FINE.

OH, ALL RIGHT... BUT DON'T DO ANYTHING CRAZY.
......
YAAAY! ALL RIGHT, THEN.

MOMO! TIME FOR THE DARK MEDICINE!!
RIIIGHT ...

WELL? WHAT'S IT TASTE LIKE?
IS IT YUMMY? DOES IT GO DOWN SMOOTHLY?
TASTES LIKE BOILED MUD AND GARBAGE!
I CAN'T...
CHUG!♪ CHUG!♪
YOU'RE ALREADY DOING SOMETHING CRAZY!

A DEMON'S EMOTIONAL SCARS

FIRST, WE NEED INTEL!
WHAT SORT OF DEMON IS POSSESS-ING YOU, MIKAN-SAN?
MY FAMILY CALLED IT "UGALLU."

A MONSTER FROM MESO-POTAMIA, NO? 'TWAS SAID TO PROTECT FAMILIES FROM EVIL IF ITS IMAGE WAS CARVED INTO THEIR ENTRY GATES.
I DOUBT 'TIS THE GENUINE ARTICLE, THOUGH.

IF 'TWERE A REAL MONSTER OF LEGEND, IT WOULD HAVE MORE POWER.
MORE LIKELY, YOUR FATHER PLACED A FAMILIAR IN A SIMILAR HOST BODY AND GAVE IT A SIMPLE COMMAND.

I SEE... SO, IT'S LIKE THAT JELLO MONSTER.
WHAT JELLO MONSTER?
A THING THAT CHASED ME NOT LONG AGO.

A MASTER BED-MAKER

FAMILIARS CAN USU-ALLY ONLY MANAGE SIMPLE TASKS, AND LACK MINDS OF THEIR OWN...
BUT UGALLU DRAWS FROM MY MAGIC POWER ...
SO IT BECAME MORE COMPLEX THAN WE EXPECT-ED.

AND SO...WE COULD NO LONGER CONTROL IT.
I KNOW MY PAPA REGRETS IT. I'D LIKE TO DEAL WITH IT MYSELF.
HEY, PITCHER, YOU SCAAARED?

UGALLU... I CAN'T TELL WHAT KIND OF SWEETS IT LIKES.
IT MIGHT BE A CARNI-VORE.
I GUESS WE'LL JUST HAVE TO GO SEE FOR OUR-SELVES!

HEY HEEEY!
OKAY, THAT MEANS IT'S FUTON TIME NOW!!
LET'S ALL LIE DOWN!
IS "FUTON TIME" AN ABSOLUTE MUST?

RELAX, IT'S THE BLUNT SIDE

WAKE UP, SHAMIKO.
MYAH ...?
IT LOOKS LIKE THOU HAST ENTERED MIKAN'S MIND.

IT'S PRETTY DARK IN HERE.
STAY CLOSE TO ME, SHAMIKO.
?!
WHAT'S THAT WEAPON?! IT'S SO DARN COOL!

UH...WHY DO YOU LOOK SO EXCITED?
DON'T GET SO CLOSE TO THE BLADE.
IT PUSHES MY DEMON BUTTONS!
SHOW MEEE!! LET ME SEEE!!

SWOOSH
YOU'RE TOO CLOSE.
I'M SORRY! I GOT CARRIED AWAY!

DEMON TUMMY-TOUCH

THE POOR VISIBILITY IS LIKELY DUE TO THE CURSE THAT HATH FUSED WITH MIKAN'S ETHEREAL BODY.
THAT WILL MAKE IT HARD TO FIND THE RIGHT LOCATION.
FIRST, THOU MUST SEARCH FOR AN AREA THAT LOOKS STRANGE.

OH, RIGHT! ARE YOU FEELING OKAY, MOMO? ISN'T YOUR TUMMY COLD?
THAT MEDICINE WAS THE GROSSEST THING EVER, BUT I'M FINE.

You'll build up resistance to the darkness-stabilizing medicine if you take it too often.
Save it for when you really need it, okay?
STILL, I CAN'T DO THIS TOO OFTEN.

Also, I billed you for the ingredients other than the jade! Thanks, Chiyoda-san!!
Receipt
FOR VARIOUS REASONS...
IT WOULD BE REALLY BAD IF WE FAIL THIS TIME.
I WONDER WHAT EXACTLY WAS IN THAT STUFF...

THE EASIEST PLACE TO GRAB

DIRECTION-CHOOSING STAAAFF!
PLUNK
LOOKS LIKE IT'S THIS WAY.
REALLY? YOU REALLY THINK THIS'LL WORK?

IT'S JUST FOR PEACE OF MIND!!
I ALSO HAVE MY SNACK-TIME STAFF.
WHAT ON EARTH?
WELL... WE CAN'T LET OUR GUARD DOWN NOW, SO I'LL HAVE THE SNACK LATER.

AH...BUT THERE'S A LIGHT OVER THERE.
ISN'T THAT--
IT'S MIKAN-SAN!

LET'S GO RIGHT--
YANK
NOT YET!!
NOT THE TAIL!

IT STILL WOULDN'T SPEAK ENGLISH

BE CAREFUL WITH MY TAIL, DARN IT!
IT WOULDN'T BE WISE TO RUSH IN LIKE THAT.
LIKE I SAID BEFORE, TAKE A GOOD LOOK FIRST.

WHAT DO YOU THINK WHEN YOU SEE THIS?
MIKAN-SAN IS SO CUTE!
INCORRECT.
YOU ARE NOW DEAD.

LOOK AGAIN. THERE'S A STRANGE BLACK FOG AROUND HER, RIGHT?
I THINK THAT'S THE CORE FORCE FIELD THAT PROTECTS HER.
FIRST, LET'S SEE IF WE CAN COMMUNICATE FROM A DISTANCE.

<EXCUSE ME!>
<I WANT TO BE YOUR FRIEND! WE ARE THE WORLD! I HAVE CAKE BOX!>
WHY DID YOU SPEAK ENGLISH?
BECAUSE THE DEMON'S FROM A FOREIGN COUNTRY!!
Demon's Dream Manju

BECOME A DEMON WHO CAN WIN PEOPLE OVER

?!
BWOOSH
I KNEW IT WOULD ATTACK US!
TRY TO TALK TO IT! I'LL STALL FOR TIME!

UM... UGALLU-SAN! MIKAN-SAN WANTS YOU TO STOP!
IS THERE ANY WAY YOU COULD COME OUT OF HER?!

'TIS NO USE. IT CANNOT SEE NOR HEAR THEE NOW!
WITHOUT A HOST BODY, UGALLU'S VERY BEING MUST HAVE MELTED INTO THAT OF MIKAN.
'TIS SENSING OUTSIDE MAGIC AND ATTACKING ON INSTINCT.

THEN, IF WE REMOVE IT ALL...
NAY, 'TIS A PARASITE. THERE IS A GOOD CHANCE THOU WOULDST SIPHON OFF MIKAN'S MAGIC.
OH NO!

SOMETIMES YOU DO RUN INTO CHAOS

FIND AN OPENING AND REMOVE THE PARASITE.
......
BUT I WAS ABLE TO CLEAN UP THE MUD IN LITTLE MOMO'S DREAM.*
WAIT A MINUTE...

"a mythical spear that can stir up chaos and give it form!!"
......
MOMO... BUY ME A LITTLE MORE TIME!

I'M GOING TO MAKE A WEAPON...
THAT CAN GIVE MELTED THINGS A SOLID FORM!
HUH?!

OVER POWERED WEAPON...
AME-NO...
NUHOKOOOO!!

* See Volume 1.

A FORM BASED ON HUMAN ENGINEERING

AME-NO-NUHOKO?!
A LEGENDARY SPEAR THAT STIRS UP CHAOS AND GIVES IT FORM!
BUT HOW CAN SHE ...

DUN-DUN-DUN!

ISN'T THAT JUST A WHISK?!
IT'S THE BEST WAY TO STIR THINGS!!

I'LL USE THIS TO SOLIDIFY THE FOG AND SEPARATE IT FROM MIKAN-SAN!
REALLY?! YOU REALLY THINK THAT'LL WORK?!

DEMON MIXER

OKAY, IT'S MIXING TIME! TIME TO SOLIDIFYYY!!
WHIRL
YEAH, WHATEVER! GUESS IT'S WORTH A SHOT.
WHIRL

AH...IS THE FOG CONDENSING? AND 'TIS GETTING BRIGHTER!

I...I DID IT! IT REALLY WORKED!
STAY BACK!
NOW IT'S... MUCH SMALLER.

WHA...?!
IT'S A GIRL?!
AND SHE'S TALKING!!

BECOME A MAGICAL GIRL WHO WEARS A SMILE WELL

SO... ARE YOU UGALLU?
NNGAH.
ME HAVE... FORM? WHY?
WHO... ARE YOU?

I'M... HERE ON BEHALF OF HINATSUKI MIKAN.
NOW WHAT?
WHAT WOULD SHAMIKO SAY?
AH...

UM...DO YOU LIKE SWEETS? I WANT TO TALK THINGS OUT WITH YOU.
IF THAT'S OKAY WITH YOU, PLEASE SIT.

NNGAH.
SO...IS THAT A YES TO TALKING IT OUT?
NNGAH.
DON'T GIVE UP, MOMO-SAN! USE YOUR SOCIAL SKILLS TO NEGOTIATE SMOOTHLY!!

PERSUASION (PHYSICAL)

SHOOM
THANK GOODNESS... DON'T THINK... UUURGH...
SHAMIKO! ARE YOU OKAY?!

I-I THINK... I USED... TOO MUCH MAGIC... YEAH.
YOU TALK TO... MIKAN-CHAN... AND THAT GIRL.
PERSUADE THEM... PLEASE...

STAAA RE...
ALL RIGHT... I'LL TRY. YOU JUST REST.
ALTHOUGH, I'M NOT A GREAT TALKER.

IF IT DOESN'T WORK, CAN I TALK WITH MY FISTS?
IT BETTER WORK!

AT SAVE
THE QWEEN

STILL NO ANSWER FROM MIKAN.
HRMM... I'M KINDA WORRIED.
Mikan
LEFT ON "READ"
KIRARA

LET THE BODIES LIE IN RUINS.
WAAAAAAAH?!
WHAT IS THIS?!

HER ADDRESS SAYS SHE LIVES HERE, BUT...
WHAT'S THIS PAPER?
WHY IS THE DOOR BROKEN?
OH WELL! 'SCUSE ME! I'M COMING IIIIN!

AN ACCIDENT?! AN ATTACK?! A PSYCHOTIC BREAK?!
SHHH!! THEY'RE IN A DREAM DEEP DIVE RIGHT NOW!!
The story so far:
We're negotiating with the demon that lives in Mikan's soul!

CROSSING AND CRASHING THE STREAMS

I FIND IT DIFFICULT TO DEPEND ON THEE HERE.
SHALL I GIVE THEE SOME ADVICE?
FINE... BACK ME UP, PLEASE.
PHEW...

HOW SWEET! I EXPECT PLENTY OF H.B.C.S LATER--
WAA-AH!! WHAT IS THIS?!
AN ACCIDENT?! AN ATTACK?!
FZZT FZZT
SHHH!! THEY'RE IN A DREAM DEEP DIVE RIGHT NOW!
LILITH-SAN?

SORRY, MOMO. 'TIS A VISITOR FLAG. DO THY BEST!!
MIC OFF!!
HUH?
"VISITOR FLAG"?

HEY!
WHAT DO WE "TALK"?
SENSE GREAT HATRED IN YOU.
DAMN HER...
AAAH, SORRY... DON'T WORRY, IT'S NOT TOWARDS YOU.
I CAN'T BELIEVE I ACTUALLY RELAXED FOR A SECOND THERE.

A MUSCLE-HEADED INFLUENCE

MEANWHILE, INSIDE MIKAN'S MIND...
YUM!
WELL, SHE DID SIT DOWN TO NEGOTIATE WITH ME.

UGALLU...
A FAMILIAR BASED ON A MESOPOTAMIAN MONSTER.
HOW CAN WE GET HER TO LEAVE IN PEACE?

LONG CLAWS...
LESS REACH THAN A SWORD, BUT SHE MIGHT HAVE PROJECTILE WEAPONS, TOO.
I CAN'T READ THE MOVEMENTS OF THE FOG AT HER FEET...
AND UNFORTUNATELY, SHE'S GOT MIKAN RIGHT BEHIND HER.

MOMO.
ART THOU, PERCHANCE, MAKING BATTLE ASSESSMENTS?
?
?!
N-NO, WE'RE GONNA TALK IT OUT!!

MIGHT MAKE SOMETHING EASY TO DIGEST

THIS'LL BE HARD WITH MIKAN BEING BASICALLY HELD HOSTAGE.
IF SHE WAKES UP, THE NEGOTIATION IS OVER.
I'D LIKE TO GET HER AWAY, FOR A START.

SWEETS GONE.
YOU HAVE... MEAT?
HUH? MEAT?

SHAMIKO, DO YOU HAVE A STAFF OF MEAT, OR SOMETHING?
WOBBLE...
I... CAN TRY.
SHAMIKO RAISES THE STAFF OF SOMETHING-OR-OTHER!

I'M SORRY... I CAN'T... DO MEAT RIGHT NOW.
A STAFF OF PORRIDGE, MAYBE?
AH... IT'S FINE. SORRY... JUST REST.
!
BUT SHE DOESN'T HAVE ENOUGH MP!

PEACH BODY LANGUAGE

YOU HAVE NO MEAT...A SHAME.
CRACKLE...
HER FORM IS STARTING TO BREAK DOWN.
I GUESS THAT MEANS THE EFFECTS OF SHAMIKO'S STAFF AREN'T PERMANENT.

LET ME CUT TO THE CHASE. CAN YOU EXTRACT YOURSELF FROM MIKAN?
YOUR WORDS TOO HARD!!
SPEAK IN SIMPLE WAY.

YOU... IF YOU LEAVE THIS BODY, YOU'LL BE FREE.
MIKAN WILL BE HAPPY, THEN WE'LL ALL PARTY.
?
UM, MOMO? YOU'RE STARTING TO SOUND LIKE A RAPPER.

THIS IS A PAIN.
IT'S SIMPLEST TO EXPLAIN WITH BODY LANGUAGE.
DON'T GIVE UP SO EASILY, DARN IT! TRY HARDER!!

THE REASON FOR UGALLU'S ACTIONS, REVEALED!

CAN'T LEAVE THIS PLACE!
ME MADE TO PROTECT MIKAN.
THIS MY JOB! THE REASON ME STAY WHOLE!

WHEN ME SUMMONED, MY HOST BODY WAS BADLY MADE. FELL APART.
BUT HERE, ME PROTECT MIKAN. EVEN WITH NO BODY.
ME NO LEAVE! NO MATTER WHAT FORM ME MUST TAKE!!

SO, HOW DID YOU DECIDE WHEN TO DEFEND HER?
CAN'T SEE OUTSIDE.
SO, ME ATTACK WHEN HER HEART TREMBLE!!

AT-TACK! AT-TACK!
MIKAN SAFE. ME GOOD!!
ME BEST DEFENDER!
THAT DOESN'T WORK AT ALL!!

PEACH TRAUMA REARS ITS HEAD

YOUR ACTIONS HAVE CAUSED LOTS OF SUFFERING FOR MIKAN.
WHEN SHE FEELS THINGS STRONGLY, PEOPLE GET HURT.
SHE'S BEEN STRUGGLING TO HOLD YOU BACK.

NNGAH!
MIKAN... HAS HURT?
YES, QUITE A BIT.
AND FOR THAT MATTER, I HAVE, TOO!

THANKS TO THE BARRIER MY SISTER MADE FOR MIKAN...
THAT TURNS THE WORST CURSES INTO FUNNY ONES...
I'VE HAD TO WEAR TONS OF EMBARRASSING COSTUMES!

FLASH
SO, ON BEHALF OF ALL YOUR VICTIMS, PLEASE APOLOGIZE TO ME!!
MOMO... THAT'LL JUST COMPLICATE THINGS. MAYBE LATER?

UGALLU, CONVINCED ①

ME... NOT DOING GOOD JOB?
AM BAD FAMILIAR?
I KNOW THAT YOUR INTENTIONS WERE GOOD...
BUT... YOU WENT ABOUT IT WRONG.

OH NO...
MY JOB... PROTECTING MIKAN.
ス...
SSHHFF...
CAUSING TROUBLE NO GOOD.

CRACKLE...
ME THINK ME MELT AGAIN SOON.
ME LEAVE BEFORE THAT HAPPEN.

THANKS FOR BEING SO UNDERSTANDING.
NNGAH!
ME A FAMILIAR! ME LIKE BEING TOLD "THANK YOU"!
ALTHOUGH, THAT WAS FIRST TIME.

UGALLU, CONVINCED ②

I'M GLAD.
THAT WENT BETTER THAN I EXPECTED. BUT--
WAIT.

YOU SAID YOUR JOB IS "THE REASON YOU STAY WHOLE," RIGHT?
WHAT WILL HAPPEN IF YOU LEAVE?

ME HAVE NO MORE ROLE.
NO JOB. NO HOST BODY.
NO MORE REASON TO EXIST.
WILL JUST DISAPPEAR.

YOU'LL DISAPPEAR?!
ME IS FAMILIAR.
NO HEART, NO SOUL. IS NORMAL TO DISAPPEAR!

EMPRESS OF DARKNESS (SMALL BUSINESS OWNER)

WAIT A MINUTE!! THAT'S NO GOOD!!
YOU CAN'T JUST DISAPPEAR!!
HOW CAN YOU HAVE NO HEART IF YOU LIKE BEING TOLD "THANK YOU"?!

WHO YOU? WHY SO WORKED UP?
I'M THE DARK EMPRESS WHO'S BEEN LYING OVER THERE!!
THE SELF-PROCLAIMED BOSS OF THIS TOWN!!

KOFF!! NOT ENOUGH STRENGTH...!
DON'T PUSH YOURSELF, SHAMIKO.
THE BOSS? REALLY?

DARK EMPRESS?
THIS GIRL WITH SKINNY LITTLE TAIL... YOUR BOSS?
TECHNICALLY, YES.

UGALLU'S REASON FOR EXISTING

I CAN'T JUST LET YOU DISAPPEAR, EITHER.
LET'S TRY TO FIND ANOTHER WAY.
BUT...

ME MADE TO PROTECT MIKAN...
BUT ME MADE MIKAN SUFFER.
MIKAN... NEVER FORGIVE ME.

?!
WHOOOSH
UGALLU-SAN?!

WAIT... WHY'S SHE FALLING APART SO FAST NOW?!
I GUESS IT'S BECAUSE SHE'S LOST HER ATTACHMENT TO HER ROLE.
WHAAAAT?!

GRABBING CHAOS FROM BEHIND

FEEL... SO WEAK...
C'MON, HANG IN THERE!!
YOUR HEART'S CLEARLY BROKEN!! THERE'S NO WAY YOU DON'T HAVE ONE!!

ME LEAVE BEFORE ME MELT.
WAS HAPPY HERE FOR WHOLE LIFE.
TELL MIKAN THANKS FOR ME.

ME WISH... ME DONE BETTER...
SO SHE THANK ME, TOO.
W-WAIT!
STOP RIGHT THERE!!

MIKAN-SAN?!
I'VE BEEN LISTENING FOR A WHILE NOW...
AND YOU NEED TO STOP TAKING THE BLAME AND BEATING YOURSELF UP!

I'M TOTALLY DEPENDABLE, RIGHT?

GOODNESS, YOU'RE HARD TO HOLD ONTO!!
STOP MELTING FOR A SECOND!!
NGA-GAAAH?!
SHE'S HOLDING ONTO CHAOS!!
GLURP
GLURP
GLURP
GLURP
GLURP

MIKAN... HOW ARE YOU HERE?
MIKAN IS HALF-CONSCIOUS RIGHT NOW.
THOU HAST EXPERIENCED IT ONCE, THYSELF.

WE HAD A SUDDEN GUEST IN THE REAL WORLD...
SO I HAD HER HELP ME WAKE MIKAN UP A LITTLE!
Should I shake her about this much, Shamisen?

WHICH MEANS I FINALLY GET TO TALK TO YOU AGAIN!
UGALLU... THIS IS AN ORDER FROM YOUR EMPLOYER.
STOP GETTING DEPRESSED AND MAKE THINGS RIGHT!

PINK HEART DAM NEAR CAPACITY

MAKE RIGHT? BUT ME DID JOB BAD.
YOU... NOT MAD?
FRANKLY, I AM!
IT'S BEEN TERRIBLY HARD FOR ME!

BUT THAT'S EXACTLY WHY...
IF YOU GET HEARTBROKEN AND MELT OVER ONE FAILURE ...
YOU'D BE GETTING OFF WAY TOO LIGHTLY!

AND BESIDES!
I FOUND FRIENDS WHO ACCEPTED ME, EVEN WHEN I MESSED UP.
SO...YOU SHOULD GIVE IT ANOTHER SHOT, TOO!!
NNGAH...

WHAT ABOUT PINK LADY?
SHE WANTED ME SAY SORRY.
SHE'S A BIG-HEARTED MAGICAL GIRL, SO DON'T WORRY ABOUT THAT!
UM, EXCUSE ME?

BECOME AN ORGANIZATION WITH GREAT BENEFITS

ALL RIGHT.
ME TRY AGAIN.
NOW, THAT'S THE SPIRIT!!

BUT WHAT ME DO NOW?
THIS FORM GONNA MELT AGAIN!!
IT WOULD BE TOUGH IN HERE.
BUT OUT IN THE REAL WORLD, THERE MIGHT BE A JOB FOR YOU.

WH-WHAT DO YOU MEAN?
WE'LL SUMMON UGALLU INTO THE REAL WORLD--PROPERLY THIS TIME--
AND GIVE HER A NEW JOB.

I CALL IT...
THE "RELAUNCH UGALLU IN TAMA CITY PROJECT"!!
RELAUNCH?!
DON'T GIVE UP, DEMON AND FRIENDS!! FIND A NEW HOME FOR THIS FAMILIAR!!

I'M SLEEEEPY!! HOW LONG DO I HAVE TO KEEP THIS UP?
I HOPE THEY'RE OKAY IN THE DREAM WORLD!
NNNH...

AAAAH!
LURCH!!
WHOA, YOU'RE AWAKE!! GOOD MORNING, SHAMIKO!!
ANRI-CHAN!!

I'M SO GLAD YOU CAME! THANKS SO MUCH!!
WHILE YOU'RE HERE, PLEASE HELP US SUMMON A NEW LIFE!!
SURE, YOU GOT IT!

WAIT A SEC!! WHAT DOES THAT MEAN?!
YOU'RE MIXING ME UP IN SOME SHADY STUFF!!
AT LEAST EXPLAIN IT FIRST!!
OF COURSE! I'M SORRY!!
SNAP

MARMALADE GIRL

TO SUM UP FAMILIARS...
THEY ARE A MASS OF MAGIC GIVEN A HOST BODY AND SIMPLE PROGRAMMING.

IT TAKETH A FAIR AMOUNT OF KNOWLEDGE AND SKILL TO MAKE THEM...
AND TO GET THEM TO UNDERSTAND THEIR ORDERS.
PERHAPS THAT IS WHERE THE HINATSUKI FAMILY FELL SHORT.
?

WITH ITS HOST'S HIGH-QUALITY MAGIC...
IT BECAMETH A STRONG AND COMPLEX BEING.
SO MIKAN RAISED AND NURTURED UGALLU-CHAN!

THAT MAKES MIKAN HER **MAMA**!!
YOU'LL HAVE TO LOOK AFTER HER.
MAMA!
COULD YOU STOP SAYING "MAMA," PLEASE?

UGALLU-CHAN IS NOT PRO-LEMON

UGALLU-CHAN THE FAMILIAR, HUH?
UGALLU WAS SUMMONED TEN YEARS AGO IN A GLITCHY STATE...
SO SHE WASN'T STABLE IN THE REAL WORLD.

Magic circle that summoned me was small and messy.
So me not really understand orders!
Host body was crummy. Couldn't use it!

But worst of all...
fried chicken offered me had no magic! Tasted like lemon!!
うがるーっ!!
UGALLUUUGH!!

Offerings are big part of starting contract!! Too gross means no power for tummy!! Who puts **lemon juice** on meat?!
Erm... I'm sorry about my family's tastes.

PEACH TACKED-ON OVERTIME

BUT...I REALLY DO WANT TO HELP HER.
ALL THIS TIME, I'VE ASSUMED SHE WAS A RATHER CRUEL CREATURE.
I THOUGHT PAPA SUMMONED THE WRONG BEING...

BUT THAT WASN'T THE CASE.
WE JUST SUMMONED HER WRONG. SHE'S BEEN TRYING HER BEST.
I'D LIKE TO GIVE HER A NEW REASON TO LIVE.

IF WE SUMMON UGALLU PROPERLY THIS TIME...
SHE SHOULD BE ABLE TO SURVIVE OUT HERE...I THINK.
I'M SLEEPY, BUT...
ALL RIGHT! I'LL HELP OUT!!

UGALLU IS HANGING ON THROUGH SHEER FORCE OF WILL.
WE'VE GOT TO FINISH THIS TONIGHT!!
AH, SO IT'S AN ALL-NIGHTER, EH?

OKAY, KIDS, LET'S ALL CALL FOR OGURA~!♪

FIRST, WE SHOULD LIST THE STEPS AND SUPPLIES WE NEED.

YOU KNOW WHO'D BE GOOD AT THIS...

YES, MAYBE WE SHOULD ASK THAT PERSON FOR HELP?

OGURA-SAAAN!
AT YOUR SERVICE!!
HUH?!

WE WANT TO MAKE A REALLY HIGH-QUALITY, LIFE-SIZED HOST BODY.
FIND THE BEST INGREDIENTS.
NO BUDGET CAP?! IS ONE HUNDRED MILLION OKAY?!
NO, IDIOT.

ON SO MANY LEVELS... WHY?
AH...I'M SORRY. WE'VE KINDA GOTTEN USED TO IT.

THE COST KEEPS RISING

I'VE OUTLINED A SUMMONING PLAN!
Ugallu Summoning Plan
* High-quality host body
* Precise magic circle
* Tasty food, full of magic (offering)

WOW, YOU'RE REALLY FAST.
HEE HEE HEE HEE-EE!
IT WAS MOSTLY DONE FOR ME IN (ELDER) CHIYODA-SAN'S NOTES.

IT SEEMS THAT SAKURA-SAN HAD A SIMILAR PLAN IN THE WORKS...
BUT SHE PUT IT ON PAUSE BECAUSE SHE COULDN'T SOLIDIFY UGALLU.
I SEE... I HAD NO IDEA.

SHE'S WRITING DIRECTLY ON THE WALL.
HEY, AREN'T YOU RENTING THIS PLACE?
HUSH! IF I GET TOO UPSET RIGHT NOW, UGALLU WILL DISAPPEAR.

A MAESTRO IN OUR MIDST

NOW, I HATE TO BE THE BEARER OF BAD NEWS...
BUT I DON'T THINK WE CAN GET ALL THE THINGS WE NEED TONIGHT.
WHA...?
NOT A CHANCE!♥

FOR ONE, WE CAN'T MAKE THE FOOD FOR THE OFFERING.
MAKING A CONTRACT WITH A FAMILIAR INVOLVES HIGH-QUALITY MAGIC COOKING.

BUT... THERE AREN'T MANY SKILLED CHEFS AROUND WHO CAN ALSO DO MAGIC.
SKILLED CHEF...
COOKING WITH MAGIC...
THEY'D HAVE TO BE A MAESTRO!
SPA-SPARKLE
SPARKLE
SPARKLE
SPARKLE

AH, I THINK ONE OF MY CO-WORKERS CAN DO IT!!
REALLY? SOMEONE IN THIS TOWN?

A WORKING DEMON WITH CONNECTIONS

BUT YOU NEED HIGH-QUALITY MEAT FOR MAGIC CUISINE!
THERE WON'T BE ANY BUTCHERS OPEN AT THIS HOUR.
ANRI-CHAN'S FAMILY SELLS MEAT.
HEYOOO~!
OH MY, REALLY?

BUT, BUT...YOU ALSO NEED TAIL FUR FROM A MYTHICAL BEAST FOR THE HOST BODY.
IT'S AN ALCHEMICAL INGREDIENT THAT'S FULL OF MAGIC.

EVEN IF WE ORDER IT ONLINE, IT'LL TAKE A FEW DAYS.
WHAT'S A MYTHICAL BEAST?
ANY LEGENDARY CREATURE THAT CAN SPEAK... AN ANIMAL-SHAPED DEMON.

AH... YUKO KNOWS ONE OF THOSE, TOO.
THE BOSS AT MY PART-TIME JOB IS AN ANIMAL DEMON.
WAIT, REALLY?

MR. JELLO'S SACRIFICE WASN'T IN VAIN

FINALLY... WE DON'T HAVE ANY SOIL FROM A SPIRITUAL SITE.
THAT MOUNTAIN YOU VISITED RECENTLY IS ONE...
BUT YOU COULD NEVER GET THERE AND BACK IN TIME.

UM...I BROUGHT SOME DIRT FROM THE MOUNTAIN BACK WITH ME.
WHAT? WHY?
TO COMMEMORATE MY VICTORY.

OH, SHAMIKO-CHAN... YOU ARE SOOO MUCH FUUUN!!
I'M SO GLAD I FOLLOWED YOU AROOOUND!!
OH, UM, SURE!!
GOMORRAAAH!

THAT'S EVERYTHING! WE CAN COMPLETE THE RITUAL TONIGHT!!
LET'S HURRY UP AND GET TO WORK!
RIGHT!!

MAGIC OVERDOSE

Café Asura
YA NEED MAGIC FOOD FOR A RITUAL?
SORRY TO BOTHER YOU SO LATE AT NIGHT.
IT'S FIIINE! I'LL HELP YA OUT. ♪

PLEASE MAKE SOMETHING A CARNIVOROUS DEMON GIRL WOULD LIKE!
OH MY, THAT'S SOME MIGHTY FINE MEAT.
THIS WILL BE FUN!

FWOO OO OO OOSH
Oh, twists of fate, let me welcome a new girl to this town...
by creating the ultimate fried dish with all my heart!

I DO BELIEVE THIS IS MY BEST WORK YET!!
IT'S SO STUFFED WITH MAGIC THAT A NORMAL PERSON WOULD FAINT DEAD AWAY!!
WILL THAT REALLY BE SAFE?

THE BOSS RUNS LOW ON BUTT FUR

SO, WHAT EXACTLY ARE YOU GOING TO DO TO ME?
WE NEED HEAPS OF YER BUTT FUR TO SAVE A LIFE, BOSS.
LICO-KUN, PLEASE PHRASE THINGS MORE DELICATELY!

I CAN PLUCK MY OWN TAIL, YOU KNOW!!
BUT YOUR BACK'S THROWN OUT, BOSS. I'LL DO IT SO YA DON'T GET HURT.
WHY DO I NEED TO BE TIED DOWN?!

I JUST LOVE YA SO MUCH, BOSS. I WANNA SEE YOU FROM EVERY ANGLE.
LICO-KUN, WE NEED TO HAVE A TALK LATER!
SNICK...
I KIND OF KNOW WHAT YOU MEAN.
ET TU, YUKO-KUN?!
SNICK...
SNICK...

LICO-KUN, STOP IT!
GAH! LICO-KUN!!
GAH!
STOP, LICO-KUN!!
AAAGH, LICO-KUUUUN!!
PLEASE ADMIRE THESE PEACEFUL FLOWERS WHILE THE BOSS'S TAIL FUR GETS PLUCKED.

RYO-CHAN GETS MOBILIZED

I GOT THE FOOD AND FUR FROM MY WORK-PLACE!
IT'S SO GLOWY!
WE'RE ALMOST DONE WITH THE MAGIC CIRCLE, TOO.
WOW, AL-READY?

CHIYODA-SAN, FINISH UP THE PAINT, PLEEE-ASE!
NEED ME TO ERASE THIS PART?
HUH?
THE FIELD DAY GIRLS?

I TEXTED THEM ABOUT THE PLAN, AND THEY ALL CAME TO HELP.
IT'S SO LATE ... BUT THEY'RE ALL HERE HELPING OUT.
DON'T CRY, OR UGALLU WILL DIS-APPEAR!

NOW, SLOWLY ADD WATER TO THE HOST BODY CLAY AND STIR. HEE HEE HEE HEE!
SIS... WHO IS THIS?
RYO'S HERE, TOO?!

A DEMON/MAGICAL GIRL COLLAB

WOW... WE REALLY GOT IT ALL DONE IN ONE NIGHT!
LET'S START UP THE MAGIC CIRCLE.
SHAMI-KO, GO AHEAD.

WHO, ME?!
UGALLU IS A DEMON, SO A DARK VESSEL WOULD BE BEST.
I'LL HELP WITH THE MAGIC SUPPLY.

I'M STILL YOUR VASSAL RIGHT NOW...I THINK.
THE DARK MEDI-CINE IS STILL IN EFFECT, BUT JUST BARELY.
A-ALL RIGHT, THEN!!

UGALLU-SAN...
COME ON DOWN!!

A NEW LIFE IS BORN

NNGAH...
ME... HAVE... A BODY.
WE DID IT! IT WORKED!!

NEW BODY FEEL GREAT!!
WHAT SHOULD I DO FOR NEW JOB?
WELL, WE'VE BEEN TALKING ABOUT IT...

AND YOU'VE GROWN TOO COMPLEX TO BE JUST A FAMILIAR.
SO... WE WANT YOU TO FIND A JOB THAT *YOU* WANT TO DO.
THAT'S YOUR NEW JOB!

MY JOB... IS TO FIND JOB??
NOT UNDERSTAND... MIGHT GLITCH AGAIN.
THAT JOURNEY IS WHAT LIFE'S ALL ABOUT!

SWEET AND SOUR MIKAN-CHAN

WILL TRY TO CARRY OUT ORDER.
ME SHOULD GO NOW.
ペコ
BOW
WHAT?! WHERE ARE YOU GOING?!

YOU HAVE NOWHERE TO LIVE, DO YOU?
MIKAN ANGRY. SHOULD FIND HOME FAR AWAY.
YOU'RE STILL SPOUTING THAT NONSENSE?!

JUST LIVE HERE UNTIL YOU FIND WHAT YOU WANT TO DO!!
YOU LIVED INSIDE ME FOR TEN YEARS! ANOTHER TEN OR TWENTY IN MY HOME IS NO BIG DEAL!!

YOU AND I ARE *FAMILY* FROM NOW ON!!
ALL RIGHT?! GET IT?!
U-UH... SURE, GOT IT.
ANOTHER NEW FRIEND HAS COME TO TOWN.

WHAT'S THE TAIL GOT TO DO WITH IT?

THEN, THE NEXT DAY...
THAT'S A NEW LOOK, UGALLU-SAN.
MIKAN CLEANED ME UP!!
BOSS! GIVE ME THING TO DO!!

PLEASE STOP CALLING ME "BOSS" JUST BECAUSE OF THAT ONE COMMENT!
MIKAN TOLD ME! YOU MIKAN'S BOSS.

YOU GATHERED PEOPLE TO HELP ME.
COULD NOT HAVE DONE IT WITHOUT YOU.
SO, YOU'RE BOSS! ME CAN TELL!!

ALTHOUGH YOUR TAIL...IS SKINNY...
AND YOU KINDA SMALL, TOO.
WE DON'T SAY THE S-WORD AROUND HERE!

A SMALL DEMON'S BIG STEP FORWARD

SO, WHAT'S OUR NEXT MOVE, BOSS?
YOU'RE MAKING FUN OF ME, AREN'T YOU?
NO, NOT AT ALL.

THAT GIRL FOUND A PLACE WHERE SHE BELONGS, THANKS TO YOU.
I THINK YOU DID EVERYTHING RIGHT.
WHAT ARE YOU DOING?
GUARDING GATE.
LOOKING BACK, THAT RITUAL WAS SO COBBLED TOGETHER IT MAKES MY TAIL STAND ON END.

WHAT'S WRONG WITH THAT?
IT'S SORT OF LIKE HOW MY SISTER DID THINGS.

EVEN IF YOU ARE KIND OF SMALL.
I KNEW IT! YOU ARE MAKING FUN OF ME!!
NO, NOT AT ALL.
DON'T GIVE UP, SHAMIKO!! KEEP MAKING A PLACE WHERE EVERYONE CAN LIVE IN PEACE!!

Seven Seas
KIRARA MENU 1488
04

SECONDS!! DEMON GIRL NEXT DOOR

(CHAPTER 44)

~ MOMO AND THE SECRET OF THE STRING ~

LET'S JUST STAY CALM AND GIVE IT OUR BEST SHOT.

UM... RIGHT.
......

I'M CURIOUS ABOUT THAT STRING, THOUGH.
HON-ESTLY, I WANNA PULL IT.
ザワ...
SHIVER...

Q. WHAT HAPPENS IF YOU PULL MOMO'S STRING?
1. HER SKIRT FALLS DOWN.
2. HER UNDIES FALL DOWN.
3. THEY BOTH FALL DOWN.
4. SORRY, IT'S JUST FOR SHOW. NOTHING FALLS DOWN.
TICK TICK TICK

EX-CUSE ME FOR A MO-MENT!
YANK
? SHA-MIKO?!

WHATEVER'S GOING ON, CALM DOWN.
I'M SORRY, MA'AM!

Q. WHAT HAPPENS IF YOU PULL MOMO'S STRING?
A. SHAMIKO'S JOINTS GET STRAINED.

SEVEN SEAS ENTERTAINMENT PRESENTS

The Demon Girl Next Door

story and art by IZUMO ITO

VOLUME 4

TRANSLATION
Jenny McKeon

ADAPTATION
Kim Kindya

LETTERING AND RETOUCH
Rai Enril

COVER DESIGN
Hanase Qi

PROOFREADER
Danielle King

EDITOR
Shanti Whitesides

PREPRESS TECHNICIAN
Rhiannon Rasmussen-Silverstein

PRODUCTION MANAGER
Lissa Pattillo

MANAGING EDITOR
Julie Davis

ASSOCIATE PUBLISHER
Adam Arnold

PUBLISHER
Jason DeAngelis

Machikado Mazoku Volume 4

Originally published in Japan in 2018 by HOUBUNSHA CO., LTD., Tokyo.
English translation rights arranged with HOUBUNSHA CO., LTD., Tokyo, through TOHAN CORPORATION, Tokyo.

Seven Seas press and purchase enquiries can be sent to Marketing Manager Lianne Sentar at press@gomanga.com. Information regarding the distribution and purchase of digital editions is available from Digital Manager CK Russell at digital@gomanga.com.

ISBN: 978-1-64827-369-8

Printed in Canada

First Printing: October 2021

10 9 8 7 6 5 4 3 2 1

FOLLOW US ONLINE: ***www.sevenseasentertainment.com***

READING DIRECTIONS

This book reads from ***right to left***, Japanese style. If this is your first time reading manga, you start reading from the top right panel on each page and take it from there. If you get lost, just follow the numbered diagram here. It may seem backwards at first, but you'll get the hang of it! Have fun!!

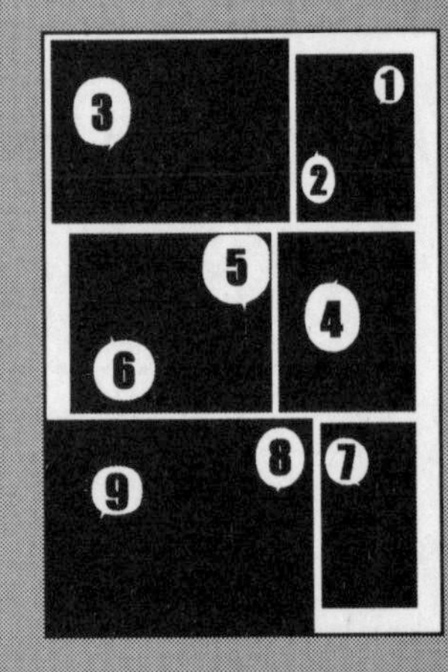
1
2
3
4
5
6
7
8
9